Foundations of
Christian Knowledge

Foundations of
Christian Knowledge

GEORGIA HARKNESS

ABINGDON PRESS
New York • Nashville

FOUNDATIONS OF CHRISTIAN KNOWLEDGE

© *MCMLV by Pierce & Washabaugh*

Library of Congress Catalog Card Number: 55-9139

SET UP, PRINTED, AND BOUND BY THE
PARTHENON PRESS, AT NASHVILLE,
TENNESSEE, UNITED STATES OF AMERICA

Foreword

THERE IS A THREEFOLD REASON FOR WRITING A BOOK ON THE foundations of Christian knowledge. In the first place, such an inquiry is basic to the total structure of Christian theology. In any quest, where one comes out is determined greatly by the choice of a route, or the routes, to be followed. Theology is no exception. Second, the crux of divergence in contemporary theology lies at this point. There are far greater areas of agreement than of disagreement among thoughtful Christians at present. But such differences as unmistakably exist, though they may appear to focus about social action or the nature of the Church or eschatology, stem for the most part from differences in grounds of authority. And third, as will be indicated in the first chapter, if the gospel of Christ is to be proclaimed with meaning and power to a confused but wistful world, it must rest on dependable foundations.

I am indebted to so many sources that it is impossible to state them adequately, but it is fitting that a special word of acknowledgment be given to two great teachers, Edgar S. Brightman and Albert C. Knudson. They laid the foundations of my mature thinking, and I owe them more than can be put in words. A second debt is to my students, who over the years have taught me much. A third is to my friend and housemate Verna Miller, who has not only typed the manuscript in the slender margins of her time but gives a practical and a spiritual undergirding to the enterprises of our common life.

GEORGIA HARKNESS

Contents

CHAPTER I

Authority in Christian Belief

THIS IS A BOOK ABOUT CHRISTIAN KNOWLEDGE. ITS TASK IS TO explore the grounds on which we can know what we know in the field of Christian truth. It could also be called a study of the grounds of authority and credibility in Christian belief—that is, of Christian apologetics.

The term "Christian knowledge" is not in very common usage. To most readers its chief context may be the name of the time-honored and long-serving missionary organization, "The Society for the Propagation of Christian Knowledge," in which the term is not used in any such specific theological sense as that in which we shall be using it. Nor is "Christian apologetics" very often talked about by this name, though some excellent books bearing this title have appeared in recent years.[1] "Christian evidences," which used to be a standard course in the curriculum of most theological seminaries, is a theme now seldom treated by this title, although, perhaps for want of a better term, the *Cumulative Book Index,* found in most libraries, still lists a lengthy assortment of books under this caption.

Nevertheless, the problems indicated by these terms are not only ancient but perennial and contemporary ones. Theologians and philosophers of religion speak much about "religious knowledge," about "reason and revelation," about "the quest for religious certainty," about "religious experience and scientific method," about the interrelationships of faith

---

[1] Notably Alan Richardson's *Christian Apologetics* (New York: Harper & Bros., 1947).

and reason and the authority of the Christian faith. It is with these problems that I shall be dealing in this book from the standpoint of the foundations of Christian knowledge.

1. *Some preliminary definitions*

Some definitions and delimitations of the area of our study may be helpful at this point. By "Christian knowledge" we do not mean the whole of Christian theology, but rather, the methods of procedure and foundations of belief which underlie the whole of it. The term "Christian knowledge" is chosen in preference to the more usual "religious knowledge," not because Christianity can fence in its claims, but because it is Christian theology for which we wish to discover valid foundations. Not religion in general (if there can be such) or a religious attitude toward life,[2] or religion in any of the other great religions such as Buddhism or Mohammedanism, but the Christian religion is what we are concerned about. A crucial problem will be the attempt to discover wherein the search for Christian knowledge has common ground with the quest for all knowledge, and within that for all religious knowledge; and wherein, if at all, the validity of Christian knowledge rests on distinctive claims.

By "Christian apologetics" we certainly do not mean to suggest apologizing for our faith, as if it were something to be ashamed of and hence must be excused! When a Christian feels that he must be either reticent or in the ordinary sense of the word apologetic about what he believes, it is a good sign that he ought to believe something else. Clarity of Christian conviction aids rather than thwarts bold witnessing. An *apologia pro fide* in the classical sense of the term is a defense of one's faith, but a defense which is at the same

---

[2] John Dewey in *A Common Faith* gave a brilliant defense of the view that while particular religions must be repudiated, "the religious" is a valid attitude.

time declaratory and explanatory. Christian apologetics aims at exposition and communication; it is the stating of the grounds of belief with the hope that there may result, if not persuasion, at least the meeting of minds in a fruitful interchange of thought. It is therefore both the search for legitimate and defensible modes of Christian thinking and the attempt to demonstrate to others the reasonableness of one's faith.

Such a study must, of course, rest on the conviction that there is some real knowledge to be acquired, something to believe that *can* be believed without self-deception. Otherwise it would savor of rationalization and psychological coercion. However, Christian apologetics as an area of theological study is not primarily an inquiry into the content of Christian doctrine; its principal concern is not *what* but *how* to believe. It must certainly have something to say about the dependability of the Bible and of the creeds of the Church as well as other sources of knowledge, but its chief concern is not whether this or that particular assertion is true. It deals rather with something that is preliminary to all such assertions: namely, the question of how we know—if we really do—what we think we know to be true.

Christian apologetics is a pursuit and mode of procedure that applies to the entire range of Christian belief. Yet it naturally comes to focus in the central affirmation of Christian faith, which is at the same time the central point of inquiry for the questioning mind, the knowledge of God.[3] "Christian apologetics deals with the question of the nature and validity of our knowledge of God, and thus compels us to examine the methods and conclusions of theological enquiry in the light of our general knowledge of the world around us and of ourselves in relation to that world." [4]

[3] Cf. the trenchant observation of William Temple, "The primary assurances of Religion are the ultimate questions of Philosophy." *Nature, Man and God*, p. 35.

[4] Alan Richardson, *op. cit.*, p. 7.

The term "Christian evidences" is so ambiguous and at points misleading that it is just as well it has dropped out of current theological usage. Sometimes it appears to be identical with Christian apologetics, and it is of some significance that the *Cumulative Book Index* previously mentioned lists all the books in the latter field under this heading. More often, however, the term "Christian evidences" has connoted, not the general structure and grounds of validity of Christian knowledge, but the particular "arguments for the existence of God," "evidences for the freedom of the will," and the like which support Christian doctrine. It thus fluctuates between epistemology, which is the study of the theory of knowledge, and metaphysics, which is the study of the nature of ultimate reality. At least partially the term has earned its disesteem by a tendency to hunt for arguments to bolster something already believed instead of engaging in an objective search for truth. When efforts to support Christian doctrine fall under suspicion of trying to "steady the ark," [5] the suspicion undercuts their supporting power.

The central problem to which we shall address ourselves in this book is the problem of authority in Christian belief, the grounds of fulfillment of the quest for religious certainty. But it must be made clear at the outset that authority is not simply another word for authoritarianism. A dogmatic insistence on adherence to traditional belief, though it may give a psychological certainty of more than a little importance to Christian experience, is no substitute for an open-minded search for Christian truth. By prejudgment of issues and refusal to look at contrary evidence, or by holding with dogmatic (even dogged) determination to views which flatly contradict each other, the quest for genuine religious certainty is cut off before it starts.

Likewise revelation, as we shall see presently, can mean

[5] From II Sam. 6:6-7.

12

a number of things, but one thing it cannot mean. To assume that God has poured some private information, some indisputable truth, into one's own mind which is not accessible to other men is to deny the possibility of revelation. That God has manifold and even particular ways of communicating Himself to individuals is not in question, but to hold that there can be a revelation of truth which is not open to all who will apprehend it is to deny that God's disclosure is in any true sense revelatory. Revelation must have an element of the "common to all" if it is to be in any valid sense "special to me." Without such open or "public" elements there could be no interchange of Christian thought.

The term "Christian faith" is commonly used in two senses, both valid but not identical meanings. Christian faith means commitment, confidence, trust, a personal attitude of being Christian, with infinite ramifications to one's total life situation if such faith is really vital. Christian faith means also, as becomes more evident when we speak of it as "the Christian faith," a body of Christian beliefs, a structure of Christian thought, the subject matter of Christian theology. The two uses of the term meet in Christian conviction, a faith to live by. It is crucially important that these two types of faith be kept in mutually supporting relations, both clear and strong, and neither substituted for the other.

Likewise "reason" has more than one legitimate meaning, though it does not mean everything, and failure to make clear in what sense the term is used introduces endless confusion. Besides the time-honored distinctions between inductive and deductive reasoning, which have more than a little bearing on the relations between scientific method and Christian doctrine, there is an even more important distinction between reason as a purely cognitive or intellectual process and the more inclusive "existential" meaning of the term in which truth is apprehended by the whole

13

person in his total situation. In the latter context, the clash between faith and reason decreases in sharpness, but at the same time the lines of legitimate and necessary demarcation become less distinct. A major problem of our study is the attempt to define these relations.

Further definition of such familiar terms as faith, reason, revelation, religious experience, and scientific method we shall defer until we come to them in sequence of discussion. In all of them the popular and obvious meaning contains important truth which must not be overlooked, but must be integrated into the total structure of Christian knowledge. But in all of them the obvious meaning is far from the whole truth. Failure to discern their meanings, and still more, their relations, is responsible for much of the skepticism, bigotry, and religious confusion of our time.

2. *The necessity of foundations*

The necessity of keeping relations, distinctions, and meanings clear may be granted, and still a question raised as to the legitimacy or necessity of the enterprise on which we are launched. "Why spend so much time on method?" it may be asked. "Why not simply discover what the Christian faith affirms, live by it, and preach it? Is not epistemology pretty barren, while the substance of Christian theology is all we are really concerned about?" Such questions are often asked by students and others who want to get on with the discovery of answers to their theological questions instead of lingering to look at signposts along the way.

This view merits sympathy, for just as in philosophy one can spend so much time and effort on epistemology that he never gets to metaphysics, so in the field of Christian thought an excessive preoccupation with theological method can pre-empt the attention that ought to be given to the great affirmations of Christian faith. Nevertheless, unless one is willing to risk affirming the wrong things, or of having what

14

he affirms fall "like a stone" on the minds of his hearers,[6] some pedestrian work in laying foundations must be done. For several reasons this is imperative.

First, it is essential to personal Christian living. Ours is an age of religious wistfulness but of great religious uncertainty. The "acids of modernity," of which Walter Lippmann wrote graphically in *A Preface to Morals* back in 1929, have continued to eat away the old securities, and in spite of a chastened and deepened liberalism and the emergence of the new orthodoxy in the seminaries, the rank and file of church members—to say nothing of those outside the churches—have a very nebulous set of ideas about the basic matters of Christian faith. Inquiries made by my students as to the theological views of laymen occasionally yield gratifying results, but more often uncover large areas of confusion and the holding of views that are self-contradictory. This is not essentially the laymen's fault, for the leaders of churches have not taken seriously enough the need of theological preaching and teaching that is at the same time vital, and "how are they to hear without a preacher?" But it is the laymen's misfortune, and when sorrow comes, when "hopes deceive, and fears annoy," or even when one simply has to live and try to be a Christian, the lack of clear conviction as to what one can be sure of undercuts vital faith.

Second, it is essential to effective witness. The first sermon recorded as being preached in the Christian Church —Peter's on the day of Pentecost—is an *apologia pro fide* by appeal to Scripture, to history, and to the mighty acts of God in Jesus Christ.[7] Other famous apologies, such as that of Justin Martyr, Origen's *Against Celsus,* Thomas Aquinas'

---

[6] Cf. Paul Tillich's description of the attempt of certain kerygmatic theologians (apparently meaning Barth) to avoid apologetics, "The message must be thrown at those in the situation—thrown like a stone." *Systematic Theology,* I, 7.

[7] Acts 2:14-36.

15

Summa Contra Gentiles, and the *Apologia pro Vita Sua* of John Henry Newman, have varying degrees of appeal to reason, but all unite reason with Christian faith and experience to defend and witness to a conviction believed to be vitally important. If the gospel is to be effective in our day, it must speak to both mind and heart and must be expressed in terms of defensible realities.

In the third place, if the rift between the secular and the Christian world is to be bridged by the exponents of Christian faith, this can only be done by a better apologetic than has thus far been generally employed. By "better" I mean both truer and more persuasive, more persuasive not because of literary or oratorical superiority but because of superior truth. Too often the tendency is not to give an apologetic but to apologize for one's faith—usually not overtly but in terms of the assumption that science has, of course, the truth and Christian belief does not conflict with it. The other extreme, a dogmatic denial of the findings of science when they conflict with something in the Bible or the creeds, is more openly unsuited to the task of bridge building; but because it is more easily discerned, it may not do as much harm as the first procedure. The only effective Christian apologetic avoids both extremes. Speaking language intelligible to the secular world and not pious cant, it finds common ground where it exists and at the same time without apology or excuse makes clear the distinctive notes in the Christian faith.

And in the fourth place, one cannot make his way effectively through the divergent strands of contemporary theology without a concern for epistemology and methodology. An obvious element in this situation is the resurgence of biblical theology without any unanimous agreement as to modes of biblical interpretation, and the presence of many pages in contemporary writings on the relations of reason and revelation. One can, of course, decide not to read the books,

16

including this one! But if one is to understand why intelligent and able theologians, equally sincere in their quest, come out with such differing views, he must understand the differences in their presuppositions and modes of procedure. Differences which appear on the surface to cause, according to temperament, either heated rejection or too easy acceptance almost always have their roots in divergence as to grounds of authority. A case in point is the vast amount of controversy that was stirred up by the theme of the Evanston Assembly of the World Council of Churches over such an apparently incontrovertible Christian affirmation as "Christ —the hope of the world." In general American liberals, recoiling from the biblical literalism of fundamentalist premillenarians, find neither truth nor value in an eschatological "second coming," while European neo-orthodox theologians, recoiling from what they regard as the man-centered and nonbiblical aspects of American thought, believe that a "final coming in glory" is the minimum essential for the faith that Christ is the hope of the world.

Such factors as these, I trust, give an adequate apologetic for apologetics. We must now take a look at the hurdles to be overcome and the assets for overcoming the liabilities.

3. Barriers

What stands in the way of Christian apologetics? There are barriers in human nature, and in the nature of the Christian faith. These are perennial obstacles not only to the spread of the gospel as an evangel but to the propagation of the faith as a system of belief. There are, in addition, obstacles peculiar to our time. At these, as well as our assets, we must look if we would be clear-sighted.

To take a look at the barriers in human nature, there is a persistent tendency to laziness, to bigotry, to skepticism, to pride and egocentricity, and to the finding of excuses to cover all these tendencies. This, of course, does not exhaust the list of human frailties, and they are not found with equal virulence in all persons. Yet these are characteristics closely related to our problem. Paul had apparently discovered them when in speaking in his Letter to the Romans of those to whom God had made Himself known through His creation but who had nevertheless rejected Him, he said that "they did not honor him as God or give thanks to him, but they became futile in their thinking and their senseless minds were darkened" (1:21). But before beginning to discuss these tendencies a warning is in order, for those to whom the gospel is meaningful are altogether too likely to be cynical about those to whom it is not. In recognizing these traits, *mea culpa* is a necessary attitude.

Laziness assails us at the point of preferring to have our thinking done for us. To try to decide what to believe about ultimate matters is strenuous, exacting, and at points painful business. Every person who has ever found his traditional, long-accepted beliefs under challenge, particularly if these beliefs were ingrained in childhood and knit about with strong emotional ties, knows that it is not an easy process to move to others. In the process there is danger of simply exchanging an old secondhand authority for a new one. It is much easier to believe "what Mother Church believes," or in the Protestant structure more often, what some beloved individual or dynamic personality believes, than to think one's way through to new ground, and only the resolute soul will make the effort. The alternatives are to go on believing in traditional patterns, to sink into a miasma of doubt, or to decide that since nobody knows anyway, it is better not to think about it. Then the last course, which looks like the simplest, leaves one floundering when a crisis exposes an inner vacuum which there is no sure faith to fill.

Bigotry or dogmatism is the attitude of one who is so

sure he is right that he will neither open his mind to a new idea nor feel charitable toward those who hold a differing view. While often linked with the laziness just referred to, it is a more commendable attitude than pure inertia, for Christian dogmatism is a recognition that there is something in the Christian faith worth clinging to and defending. Yet when it expresses itself either in deliberate unwillingness or in psychological inability to get another's point of view, it not only cuts off the quest for truth but often breeds unloving and hence unchristian attitudes. Though it is a particular characteristic of the fundamentalist mind that stakes its faith on the literal inerrancy of the Bible, there are dogmatic liberals as well. In any case there are dogmatism and smug complacency, with animadversions against both fundamentalist and neo-orthodox Christians, among many who call themselves liberals, although it may be doubted whether true liberalism and bigotry can ever lie in the same bed.

Ostensibly the opposite of bigotry is skepticism. Actually it is possible to be as bigoted and dogmatic in what one doubts as in what one affirms. To declare that there is no evidence for the existence of God, and hence an intelligent person must be an atheist or at best an agnostic, is simply to declare that one's intellect has a blind spot toward one side of the evidence. There is a legitimate—indeed, a necessary—place for doubt in any growing mind. Without some doubt as to the validity of what appear to be fixed ideas, there could be neither advance beyond them nor rational substantiation of them. What the poet Tennyson said of his friend Arthur Hallam epitomizes the process of creative growth:

> Perplext in faith, but pure in deeds,
>   At last he beat his music out.
>   There lives more faith in honest doubt,
> Believe me, than in half the creeds.

He fought his doubts and gather'd strength,
  He would not make his judgment blind,
  He faced the spectres of his mind
And laid them; thus he came at length

  To find a stronger faith his own.[8]

However, to doubt simply for the sake of doubting or to reject old beliefs without trying to build more substantial foundations will never lead to creative fulfillment in the quest for truth.

I mentioned as barriers pride and egocentricity. It is a common contention of the neo-orthodox school of Christian thought that human sin, with its primary focus in pride, self-righteousness, and rebellion against God, corrupts not only Christian living but also Christian faith and hence makes reason theologically undependable.[9] While in my judgment this can be carried too far toward the depreciation of reason as a guide to Christian truth, there is a significant element in this contention. When a person thinks that he knows enough about the Christian religion, or that all he needs to know is discoverable through rational inquiry, the resulting attitude is one of smugness and complacency that curtails the effort to inquire. A particular instance is found in the tendency to be skeptical of everything religious while credulous of everything claiming to be scientific. This is usually accompanied, from another angle, by the tendency to reject the corporate witness of the Church as having any significance while accepting without question the results of a corporate quest for truth in the field of science.

These personal factors come to focus, usually unconsciously, in the formation of rationalizations, excuses, alibis. The

[8] *In Memoriam,* XCV.
[9] For a spirited defense of this position see Emil Brunner, *The Scandal of Christianity;* for an equally spirited protest, L. Harold DeWolf, *The Religious Revolt Against Reason.*

Christian faith not only calls for thought, but what is more difficult and exacting, for transformation of life. It challenges selfishness and sin; calls men to repentance; offers salvation which, though freely given in divine mercy, has to be accepted in contrition, humility, and redirection of will. It is easier to slough this off as "emotionalism" than to let one's emotions be purged to the point of saying with humble hopefulness, "Lord, I believe; help Thou mine unbelief." This process of evasion is seldom recognized in one's self and where recognized, seldom admitted.

But it is not alone in the frailties of human nature that the difficulties of formulating and promulgating a Christian apologetic are located. An inherent difficulty lies in the necessity for the interweaving of subjective with objective factors in the discovery of Christian truth. As noted above, revelation must have an element of the public, openly accessible approach to truth, or it is not in a true sense revelatory. Private reason is a contradiction in terms; nothing can be debated on rational grounds unless there is potentially a meeting of minds. The quest for Christian knowledge must therefore rest on objective grounds—not in the sense that the discovery of rocks, trees, tables, chairs, and other physical objects are open to all, but in the sense that anyone who takes the trouble and meets the necessary conditions can find it. On the other hand, all religion, including the Christian religion, has to be a personal experience, or it is not in a true sense religious. It can be cultus, social behavior, an element in the prevailing mores, without being a personal apprehension of the divine. A personal experience of God is not all of one mold; such relationships with deity vary widely not only in degree and intensity but in manner, hence the "varieties of religious experience." Yet some sort of religious experience is the minimum essential for the living faith that is basic to the discovery of Christian truth.

A perennial problem in Christian apologetics is the difficulty
—indeed, at some points the impossibility—of making the
Christian faith as an objective system of belief seem persuasive to one who does not accept the claims of Christ upon
his personal faith and loyalty.

More obvious than these considerations is the plain fact
that Christian theology is not an easy field in which to find
one's way around. Anything which deals with the invisible
and the imponderable is bound to be hard to grasp, and this
the Christian faith does. This is true despite the fact that the
Christian gospel in which it centers has an extraordinary
simplicity. In Jesus' time "the common people heard him
gladly," and through the centuries since common people
have believed, lived by this faith, and witnessed to it. The
Bible has been more widely read than any other book ever
written, and if we include its Sunday reading in the churches,
this is still the case. Yet Christian knowledge, whether derived from the Bible or elsewhere, is not self-evidently persuasive. Almost everybody asks theological questions—about
the meaning of life, about God, about the foundations for
right moral living, about the presence of evil, the fact of
death and what lies beyond it. But many who without knowing it have a deep interest in theology veer away from it
when it is labeled, because it suggests to them something
very abstract and very difficult.

To these problems must be added one which is less inherent but which raises barriers to their solution, the lack
of agreement among Christian theologians and churches.
That the theologians should have differences of opinion is
only natural, and is on the whole more conducive to creative
interchange of thought than to despair. Yet these differences
are inevitably confusing to laymen. And when to such differences is added the divisions among churches, the difficulties increase. In part denominational divisions stem from

theological factors, particularly at the point of the nature of the Church and the authority of its ministry and the sacraments; in larger part they are the product of nontheological factors, such as racial, national, economic, or cultural divisions. Where they exist, whatever the cause, they make the task of Christian apologetics more difficult by presenting to the world a divided front. The modern ecumenical movement has gone far toward the analysis by leaders of the grounds of difference; it has achieved more than a little, particularly through the many agencies of the National Council of Churches, in the way of co-operative effort. It can hardly be said yet to have gone far enough in the local scene so that the churches proclaim their faith to the world with a united voice.

Other barriers of a more specialized nature arise from particular presuppositions and types of philosophy which are antithetical to the Christian faith. Among these are *materialism,* which, when it is thoroughgoing (as it seldom is), leaves no place for spiritual values; *naturalism,* which admits the presence of spiritual values but finds their source and explanation entirely within the observable world of physical and human nature; *agnosticism,* which questions the possibility of any religious knowledge except as a description of the various forms of religious behavior; *relativism,* which rejects the existence of all absolutes, and hence the objective reality of God as source and ground of values; *humanism,* which often attempts to keep the moral imperatives of Jesus intact while rejecting their foundation in the God whom he worshiped and served; *logical positivism,* which so narrows the field of philosophy as to eliminate not only Christian and other religious knowledge, but all metaphysical affirmations. I shall have occasion later to show how these rival philosophies cut the ground from under the Christian faith by resting on adverse presuppositions. To the extent that they are prevalent

—and some of them, particularly naturalism, relativism, and humanism, are very prevalent—Christian faith has a hard battle to fight. Without an adequate apologetic, it loses.

4. *Resources*

Confronted by such a formidable array of obstacles, one feels tempted either to fall back on easy dogmatisms or in Voltairean terms to "cultivate one's garden." [10] But the obstacles are not the whole of the situation. There are, on the other hand, resources in human nature, in our social situation, and in the nature of the Christian faith.

The most fertile resource in human nature is the difficulty any thoughtful person finds when he tries to evade the ultimate questions of our existence. Reference has been made to the tendency of almost everybody to ask theological questions. Life forces them upon us. Whence? why? whither? *cui bono?* These are recurrent themes not only of philosophy but of the literature of the ages where human passions, joys, sorrows, and yearnings are reflected. Psychiatrists have continually to deal with personal maladjustments which stem from distorted or too nebulous beliefs about the ultimate grounds of human security. While Christian faith is not the only foundation of happy and effective living, or its presence a guarantee of it, the correlation between a vital and intelligent faith and personal stability is too great to be accidental.

There is, furthermore, in our time a growing mood of interest in theological questions. This is indicated in a variety of ways. There is, for one thing, a resurgence of interest in the Bible. Over 2,500,000 copies of the Revised Standard Version of the Bible have been sold, and while obviously not all of these have been read with understanding, the Bible remains the world's best seller. Even the controversy

[10] In *Candide,* after Pangloss has tried by a *tour de force* to justify the ways of Providence in such a way as to solve the problem of evil.

stirred up by it, stemming from theological presuppositions that resisted even linguistic change in the fear that ideas might have to be altered, is an evidence of the tenacity of theological interest. A million-dollar project, *The Interpreter's Bible,* to which the best minds in biblical scholarship and expository preaching are contributing under the general editorship of George Buttrick, is in process of consummation. In the field of general literature, the volume of book sales is a telling evidence of where public interest lies, and religious books continue to be best sellers.[11] Most of these are not ostensibly theological, but stem out of theological convictions which merge with literary skill to give them power.

In the field of books overtly theological, there are also signs of promise. Only a few years ago it was very hard to find a theological book written simply enough for laymen to grasp without special training; within the past decade a dozen or more have appeared.[12] Among the books written primarily to be read by Christian scholars, there is no less diversity than formerly, but more charity. At least among liberal and neo-orthodox writers there is less of polemic, more willingness to grant the possibility of a truth greater than the grasp of any one mind or school. Liberalism, far from being as defunct as some assume it to be, has been greatly deepened and brought closer to the main stream of Christian biblical theology, while European neo-orthodox

[11] Eugene Exman, religious-book editor of Harper & Bros., in an article entitled "Reading, Writing and Religion," in *Harper's Magazine,* May, 1953, cites some amazing evidences of this fact. In 1949, four of the five best-selling nonfiction titles were religious. In 1952 the Revised Standard Version of the Bible was printed in a million-copy first edition, an all-time record, but this was not enough to meet the demand. Books by Fosdick, Trueblood, Peale, Stanley Jones, Fulton Oursler, and Fulton Sheen, all at least partially theological in content, the religious novels of Lloyd Douglas and Sholem Asch, and the sermons of Peter Marshall have had very extensive sales.

[12] The most useful of these are listed in the Bibliography, p. 155.

leaders have lost much of their former social unconcern. This is not only a very interesting but a productive theological era.

Other currents of thought, not in themselves essentially theological, have had important theological repercussions. One of these is the emergence of Communism as a world force, which is widely recognized as being not only a form of political and economic control but a rival faith. Few who sense its evils could define the differences between its presuppositions and those of Christianity, but the more clearly these are seen, the more intelligently and the less hysterically it is opposed. Within university and other intellectual circles, naturalism and the mood of empirical positivism, though still flourishing, pre-empt the ground less completely than formerly, and the older mechanistic naturalism has largely given way to an organismic type more favorable to religious truth. A new interest in the philosophy of history, and a serious reckoning with the religious implications of Arnold Toynbee in *A Study of History,* have helped to shift the mood of thoughtful opinion closer to the presuppositions of Christian faith.

Beyond the perennial traits of human nature and this changing social climate lie resources imbedded in our faith itself. It is because of these that it is able to speak with power to the people of any age when presented vitally, intelligently, truly—and hence persuasively. What the Christian faith affirms about God, man, Jesus Christ, salvation, prayer and providence, Christian living, victory over death, and assurance of eternal life speaks to our human situation in every time and place and social environment. It calls us to battle against evil, gives comfort and power in adversity, adds enrichment to happy and ordered living. It assures to modern man, as to his fathers, the infinite resources of God if he will pay their price in humble obedience and open-minded, openhearted search.

Because the Christian faith has so much to offer, no Christian—whether layman, minister, or theologian—ought to be content to offer it in less than its truest and most persuasive form. This is why we must take very seriously the question of authority in Christian belief.

CHAPTER II

Philosophy and Theology

WE NOTED IN THE PREVIOUS CHAPTER THAT CHRISTIAN APOLO-
getics has a twofold task: to determine the grounds of authority on which the Christian faith rests and to proclaim this faith
to one's generation with the persuasiveness of credibility. We
must now look more specifically at the first of these ob-
jectives.

Three convergent but disparate areas which seek to discover truth are philosophy, science, and theology. Philosophy
is the study of the structure of reality as a whole and of the
categories of relationship between parts which give meaning
to the whole. Science as a method means empirical inquiry
aimed at the discovery of facts in any area of observable
reality; particular sciences are specialized investigations and
compilations of related data within chosen fields. Theology is
the systematized correlation of what is believed to be true
in the field of a particular historic religion; Christian theology
is systematized belief within the area of the Christian religion.

From these preliminary definitions it is apparent that
theology touches both philosophy and science but is identical
with neither. *How* it touches them, and is differentiated from
them, are crucial matters which cannot be put in a sentence.
We shall devote a chapter to each, beginning with philosophy,
which is the more inclusive and the more closed related field.

1. *The meaning and aims of philosophy*

Philosophy we have defined as "the study of the structure
of reality as a whole." But since the whole is made up of an
infinite number of parts, and these parts are put together

in relationships which the philosopher assumes to have some meaningful pattern instead of being an inchoate jumble, we added the second half of the definition, a study "of the categories of relationships between parts which give meaning to the whole." Philosophy is the study of ultimates, but not of ultimates in abstraction; rather, of ultimate meanings, sources, goals, in relation to whatever concretely exists. To be a philosopher, as Plato put it in classic terms, is to be the spectator of all time and all existence. Socrates defined the purpose of the philosopher's inquiry when he said that the unexamined life is not worth living. In a quite different context Matthew Arnold stated the goal of the philosopher's quest in his tribute to one "who saw life steadily, and saw it whole." [1]

The central concern of philosophy is metaphysics, the study of the basic nature of that which is. Included in philosophy, however, are epistemology, which deals with the principles of knowledge, and the normative sciences of logic, ethics, and aesthetics, concerned respectively with standards of right judgment in regard to the true, the good, and the beautiful. While philosophy by its very nature veers away from specialization, metaphysics may itself be viewed from certain quasi-specialized angles—ontology, or the study of the nature of being; cosmology, the study of the nature of the cosmos; axiology, the study of values. There is also a philosophy of every main field of inquiry, such as the philosophy of history, literature, science, politics, or religion.

Thus it appears that while a philosopher may direct his attention to this or that aspect of reality, for it is impossible to look at or talk about everything at once, he is under obligation not to neglect the relations of anything he is concerned about to the underlying ground of everything. If like the

[1] "To a Friend."

logical positivist he denies the possibility of sound metaphysical knowledge, his denial is one way of dealing with metaphysics. The philosopher's quest is therefore marked by a union of concern for ultimacy with universality. It is his obligation *not* to be a specialist in the sense in which a scientist is, for the philosopher "specializes in the universe."

A second important trait of philosophy is its mood of objective detachment. The philosopher, like the scientist, aims to put away all preconceptions and emotionally grounded preferences and to draw his conclusions rationally from whatever evidence—and only from the evidence—that the universe presents. Actually a philosopher or a scientist, like a theologian, is a human being who cannot help having some personal desires and interests, and these inevitably slant the direction of his inquiry, determine what he thinks important, and hence modify his conclusions. But though the philosopher may grant the necessity of some presuppositions, his aim is not to let anything in his personal loves and loyalties—or in his antipathies—affect his judgment. He endeavors, qua philosopher, to have one commitment only: namely, commitment to the search for truth.

A third characteristic of philosophy stems from the second: namely, reliance upon reason whenever reason confronts conflicting claims. This does not mean a wholesale rejection of faith, for everybody must have faith in something to live with sanity, and whether intentionally or not, a philosopher's faith appears in his chosen system. Yet faith, as an approach to truth, must always be held under surveillance if not suspicion. Philosophy views human faiths, religious and otherwise, as part of the data which existence presents. Yet to adopt any one of them as an aspect of philosophical method is to forsake the path of pure philosophy. Therefore, even in ethics and axiology, where personal faiths and commitments are essential to having anything to talk about, the philosopher's aim is not to let his own faith interfere with his rational judgment in the appraising of the human situation.

A fourth characteristic emerges logically from the second and third. The philosopher aims to avoid being an evangelist for his views. He states them, to be sure; otherwise we should not have the thousands of philosophy books that have been written through the centuries. But he aims to state them without heat, and only with such light as shines from clear statement of their own inherent truth. The philosopher is concerned that other people understand him, but not that they agree with him. Indeed, he is not always concerned to be understood, if he thinks he has something to say that can best be said in a new vocabulary or in cryptic terms. Philosophers, being human beings, like to be agreed with, and not a few have drawn disciples about them. Yet the philosopher is at this point typified less by Plato in the Academy or Aristotle in the Lyceum than by Socrates, dying without rancor when his truth is rejected, or by Spinoza, writing in lonely isolation to be read with appreciation only by later generations.

Philosophy, then, is a search for the ultimate meaning, source, and goal of all that exists, pursued with objective detachment and subordination of personal interests, in primary reliance upon reason, and without concern for persuasion except as truth when discerned is its own apologist. It must constantly be held in mind that this is the philosophical *ideal*. Philosophers, being men and women, and not themselves ideal beings, never completely conform to it. But by these canons the philosophic quest may be judged, and a philosopher is justified in charging himself or another with defection when there is deviation from it.

2. *The meaning and aims of theology*

Theology was defined above as "the systematized correlation of what is believed to be true in the field of a particular historic religion." Christian theology—which I shall hereafter mean when I say simply "theology"—is therefore "systematized belief within the area of the Christian religion." By "systematized belief" I do not necessarily mean something solidified in creeds, though this is one kind of theology. Systematization of belief is a dynamic process, and theology in its most living forms is a continual pursuit of truth. However, the stance which basically distinguishes it from philosophy is that it deals with the faith of the Christian community—always in some respects an inherited faith, although the work of reconstitution and critical judgment is an ongoing process which reinterprets, sifts, and transmits this faith.

How is theology related to philosophy? To answer this question, it must be noted that there are two main types of theology which vary according to the primary sources of Christian knowledge. These used to be called natural and revealed theology, though the more common terms now are philosophical and biblical theology.

These pairs of terms are not quite identical. To begin with the second, revealed theology does not necessarily limit revelation to the Bible, and biblical theology does not rely exclusively on revelation. These distinctions we must observe more closely in later chapters. However, biblical theology centers in the revelation of God as found in the Bible and may for most purposes be equated with what used to be called revealed theology.

Natural theology is a term in more current usage, but not always with a single meaning. As the object of attack by champions of the Reformation doctrine of *sola scriptura,* it means sometimes one thing, sometimes another. It may mean what the term itself implies—a doctrine of God directly inferred from the phenomena of nature, without reference to religious experience. Or it may be used as the equivalent of the philosophy of religion, an analysis of the common elements in the religious experience of mankind. In either case the approach is philosophical rather than biblical, and its object is to go as far as possible in affirming what is open to the observation of all and hence persuasive to the secular as well as to the religious mind.

The point of view from which this book is written is the possibility and the necessity of a synthesis of philosophical and biblical theology. Neither alone is adequate; neither one ought to be neglected or rejected. While philosophical theology puts its major accent on reason and biblical theology on faith, both faith and reason are necessary—and both are essential to meaningful conclusions by either route. There are a few contemporary theologians, Karl Barth being the most notable example, who deny that philosophical or natural theology has any legitimate place whatever in relation to Christian truth.[2] The current mood in theology, not only in Europe but also in America, accents biblical above philosophical theology, and this is a wholesome move toward a better understanding of the primary sources of our historic Christian faith. Nevertheless, most theologians recognize that there is a place for both approaches and attempt some kind of synthesis.

How to get them together is too large a question to answer here, for it is the main theme of this book. At this stage I can merely point out that there are these two general modes

[2] When asked to give the Gifford Lectures—this foundation having been established by Lord Gifford for the presentation by distinguished scholars of the grounds of natural theology—Barth accepted with the explanation that his addresses fell under the terms of the lectureship by virtue of the fact that at every point he would refute the claims of natural theology, and therefore would provide a background against which natural theology could react. *The Knowledge of God and the Service of God,* Lecture I.

of approach to the discovery of Christian truth. One is by the philosophical route of examining the totality of existence to see what evidence is presented as to the existence and nature of God, the spiritual nature of man, the nature of human society, the possibility and actuality of a God-given destiny for the individual soul and for the human race. In so far as this is a search for the conclusions to be drawn from the common characteristics of religious experience as a whole, it is called the philosophy of religion; where it is a philosophical examination of the affirmations of historic Christianity, it is philosophical theology. It is with the latter that we are here mainly concerned. The other approach is to go to the Bible to discover there the record of God's dealings with a particular people in history; His incarnation of Himself in a historic person called Jesus of Nazareth; the life, ministry, teaching, death, and resurrection of this God-man as incarnate Lord; the founding of the Christian Church in the faith that His Risen Presence makes unique demands upon His followers and offers in a unique way salvation from sin and death.

These approaches meet in the fact that the concern of both is for the discovery and validation of the basic concepts of the Christian faith as this has been mediated from the first century to the twentieth through the Christian community. If it is *Christian theology,* and not simply philosophy of religion in general or metaphysics, that we are dealing with, it is the Christian idea of God, the Christian view of man, the Christian moral imperative, the Christian concept of salvation, the Christian view of human destiny, that is under consideration. This is true whether the approach is primarily through philosophical or biblical theology, though the elements stressed will vary according to the approach. Indeed, the brief listing of topics of concern in the previous paragraph suggest that not only in terminology but also in emphasis the two types, though convergent, follow a different route.

3. *The tension between philosophy and theology*

At a very important point, both types of theology have a meeting point with philosophy, causing thereby possibilities of cordial agreement and also of tension. Both philosophy and theology deal with the ultimate grounds, meanings, sources, and goals of all that is. Theology may arrive by a more circumscribed route, but its chief concern is God, and God is not God unless He is the object of our ultimate concern and the ultimate source of our being.

Religious experience, out of which theology takes its rise, is not the whole of life. Nevertheless, it relates to the whole of life. A partial or fragmentary religion, such as the mere performance of conventional acts of worship or a humanistic attempt to live well without God, can only with serious question be called religion at all, and certainly it is not the Christian religion. Christianity summons men to a total devotion to God and offers from God both ultimate support and the only ultimate explanation of the world's existence and meaning.

Thus it appears that both theology and philosophy, at the most crucial point, have the same object of concern. In glancing at the various branches of philosophy listed above, it was doubtless apparent that metaphysics and the philosophy of religion impinge most directly on the field of theology. But there is not one of them that does not touch it with interlocking relationships. Epistemology and logic have their place in theology as in philosophy, as we must presently discern at greater length; ethics is a large part of the Christian imperative; Christian art both contributes to and must be judged by the canons of aesthetics. Theology like philosophy has a profound concern with Being, with the source and structure of the cosmos, with the problem of what is of greatest worth in the human enterprise. Every specialized branch of philosophy, though it may proceed in some areas without saying anything about God, is bound sooner or later either to meet or deliberately to bypass the question of the relation of the human enterprise to deity.[3]

With such common ground to work in, there must be either agreement or tension; there cannot be—except at the cost of leaving out something important—indifference. Thus it comes about that the greatest names in philosophy, from Socrates and Plato onward, have had a place for God, though not always for the personal and living God of Christian faith. The Bible, though not essentially philosophical in its approach, not only deals with themes of primary concern to philosophy, but it shows a deep respect for human reason. Early in the history of Christianity the Christian apologists identified Christ with the *Logos spermatikos* present also in the Greek philosophers, and the first great systems of Christian theology, in the school of Alexandria, were based upon this view.[4]

In our own time, though the resurgence of biblical theology and the emergence of the neo-orthodox school with its major stress on faith have led some to cast aspersions on philosophical theology, there are very fruitful movements which center in the search for a dynamic synthesis. Certain great books of the recent past, though their authors are no longer with us, stand as landmarks in this field. Among them

[3] Cf. Charles Hartshorne and William L. Reese, eds., *Philosophers Speak of God,* an anthology of selections from fifty great philosophers of diverse traditions (Chicago: University of Chicago Press, 1953).

[4] Justin Martyr says of Christ that he is "the Word [Logos] of whom the whole human race are partakers, and those who lived according to reason [logos] are Christians, even though accounted atheists. Such among the Greeks were Socrates and Heraclitus, and those who resembled them." *Apol.* I. 46.

Cf. also Clement of Alexandria, "The Greek philosophy, as it were, purges the soul, and prepares it beforehand for the reception of faith, on which the Truth builds up the edifice of knowledge." *Stromata* VII. 3.

are F. R. Tennant's *Philosophical Theology,* D. C. Macintosh's *Theology as an Empirical Science,* Eugene W. Lyman's *The Meaning and Truth of Religion,* William Temple's *Nature, Man and God,* and most of the books of Edgar S. Brightman.[5] Current writers making major contributions to this approach are Paul Tillich and Nels F. S. Ferré, and it is the point of view which underlies the widely circulated books of D. Elton Trueblood.

The concern for ultimacy in both philosophy and theology ensures that the fields must meet, even when their exponents choose to stand outside speaking distance. But concern for ultimacy is not the only aspect of either enterprise. Other characteristics make some tension inevitable, though this tension may be either creative or disruptive according to the personal capacity of the philosopher or theologian to see sympathetically into what both fields have to offer.

We saw that it is the aim of the philosophical method and spirit to examine the universe as far as possible with objective detachment, to rely on "the natural light of reason" and not on faith, to avoid any extrinsic appeals in the attempt to induce others to accept one's views. Can theology do the same?

The answer is yes and no. A theologian is not obligated to be evangelist. His function as a theologian is primarily to discover and systematize Christian truth, not to win souls to Christ or reform the social order. As a man and a Christian he may feel impelled to do both, but it is not these concerns which make him a theologian. Thus far he goes with the objective detachment of the philosopher. (It may be that the tendency to avoid emotional appeal is one reason

[5] Henry Nelson Wieman and Charles Hartshorne are philosophers whose systems at some points lend support to the affirmations of Christian theology, at others diverge. Dr. Brightman, though a philosopher rather than a theologian, held a view more congruent with the main stream of historic Christian faith.

why both theological and philosophical works so often seem dull to the general reader!) But when this admission has been made, it still remains true that there is an inevitable tension between philosophy and theology.

This tension roots in the fact put pointedly by Archbishop Temple in words already quoted, "The primary assurances of Religion are the ultimate questions of Philosophy." [6] To this may be added another trenchant statement from the same source, "The heart of Religion is not an opinion about God, such as Philosophy might reach as the conclusion of its argument; it is a personal relationship with God." [7]

Theology, whether philosophical or biblical, deals through and through with religion, and the Christian religion comes always as an inherited faith—a faith mediated to the present through centuries of experience in the Christian Church. It is this "given" faith—whether given through the Bible, the creeds of the Church, or living Christian fellowship—which the theologian must start with. It is this faith he must examine and then affirm, deny, or modify as the result of his inquiries. The philosopher too has a past and a starting point with presuppositions drawn at least partially from this past; but it is his aim to make his quest as independent and *de novo* as possible. The theologian, on the other hand, starts from the primary assurances grounded in the faith of the Christian community. Without this faith he would have nothing to theologize about.

Faith, we noted in the previous chapter, means something to believe and something to live by—an intellectual structure and a personal commitment. In the second sense as well as in the first, the mood of theology differs from that of philosophy. The theologian may or may not be a preacher, but he cannot adequately grasp the Christian faith from the

[6] *Nature, Man and God*, p. 35.
[7] *Ibid.*, p. 54.

inside unless he is a Christian. And if he cannot see it from the inside, he cannot see it as it is, for the Christian faith is *par excellence* that which lays claim upon one's total life and loyalty and calls one to be a servant of God and follower of Jesus Christ.

Thus it comes about that it is not easy, and in some respects it is impossible, to be at the same time a philosopher and a theologian. One may be competently trained in both fields, and speak or write sometimes in the one capacity and sometimes in the other. One may be a philosophical theologian and stand "on the boundary" (a term of which Paul Tillich makes much use in describing his own position.) [8] One may work out a "method of correlation" between reason and faith, and between living experience and Christian truth, as Professor Tillich[9] does and as this book in less elaborate fashion will attempt to do. Thomistic or personalistic philosophy can give large support to the affirmations of Christian theology. Nevertheless, one must take his stand in one field or the other, and the way he proceeds in his attempted correlations will be determined by his stance.

Theology cannot do duty for philosophy or philosophy for theology. Each suffers when the attempt is made to substitute the one for the other. Yet each can render large service to the other. At some of these contributions we must now look.

4. *The contributions of philosophy to theology*

If this were a book in metaphysics, it would be advantageous to trace the very large debt which Western philosophy owes to the thought patterns of Christianity. This debt is, of course, most conspicuously evident in medieval philosophy, and it is one of the weaknesses of philosophy as it is taught in most colleges and universities that relatively so

[8] *The Interpretation of History*, pp. 3-73, gives the fullest elaboration of what he means by the term, but he retains it also in his *Systematic Theology*.
[9] *Systematic Theology*, pp. 59-66 and throughout Vol. I, Part I.

little attention is given to the history of philosophy in the fifteen hundred years between the decline of Roman Stoicism and the appearance of Descartes. Much that is sound and true in medieval thought receives short shrift, not only because of the pressure of time in a college year, but because to the professor in charge it has an unpleasant *odium theologicum*. But it is not alone the medieval period, it is the entire Western world that has been impregnated with Christian influence. Speaking of the dream of a "Christian philosophy," Professor Tillich says:

> The term is ambiguous. It can mean a philosophy whose existential basis is historical Christianity. In this sense all modern philosophy is Christian, even if it is humanistic, atheistic, and intentionally anti-Christian. No philosopher living within Western Christian culture can deny his dependence on it, as no Greek philosopher could have hidden his dependence on an Apollonian-Dionysian culture, even if he was a radical critic of the gods of Homer.[10]

However, because this is not a book of philosophy but of theology, we shall look rather at the contributions of philosophy to theology. I agree further with Professor Tillich that "the idea of a 'Christian philosophy' in the narrower sense of a philosophy which is intentionally Christian must be rejected." [11] Philosophy cannot rest its case on the demands—whether true or false—of Christian faith. But philosophy and theology can influence each other, each remaining sovereign in its own field. What influence, then, from philosophy can properly be brought to bear upon theology?

These contributions appear primarily, on the one hand, as a spirit and mood; on the other, as epistemological method for the discovery of all knowledge including religious knowledge.

[10] *Ibid.*, p. 27.
[11] *Ibid.*, p. 28.

The basic spirit of philosophy is an open-minded search for truth. To be philosophical about anything is not only to be thoughtfully calm and unperturbed, as in the popular use of the term, but to be receptively open-minded to whatever truth can be discovered, and tolerant of differing opinions. There are, to be sure, dogmatic philosophers, flippantly and even viciously intolerant of views other than their own. I have even heard some of them "slay" inquiring youth who were trying desperately to cling to some vestiges of their inherited Christian faith! But such a mood of dogmatism or attack is not the true philosophic mood. The person who is philosophical in spirit as well as by profession has a humble and inquiring mind, with readiness to change his mind when new grounds of truth present themselves. A bigoted philosopher is a contradiction in terms.

As we have noted repeatedly, theology roots in faith, and faith means commitment as well as belief. Commitment and belief meet in convictions. A theologian must have convictions, and these ought not to vary with every "wind of doctrine." However, the peril of having convictions is that, because they are precious, they are too easily linked with bigotry. What seems in another to be "pig-headedness," stupid obstinacy, inflexible bigotry, seems in one's self to be merely standing by one's convictions! It is at this point that the philosophic spirit is needed, not only in philosophical theology but in biblical as well, to make one open to new interpretations, charitable toward those who think otherwise, restrained in polemic, and forceful in witness to what is believed to be Christian truth.

But "Christian truth" is another ambiguous term. Is there any? No, if what is meant by it is something which is the exclusive prerogative of Christianity, fenced off from assault by philosophy or the sciences. Yes, if what is meant by it is a body of distinctive truths about Christianity and the Christian faith. To get at Christian truth in the latter sense, which is the primary business of theology, it is essential to appropriate the canons of judgment by which in any field knowledge is discerned and true ideas distinguished from false ones. This matter of epistemological method is the second major contribution of philosophy to theology. It is so large a matter that we must now consider it at some length.

5. *The presuppositions of knowledge*

What are the general presuppositions of knowledge—not religious knowledge only, or Christian knowledge only, but any knowledge? If Christian theology is to have anything either to believe with certainty or to communicate to other thinking persons, it cannot build a fence around itself. Much as it is obligated to take its start from an inherited faith mediated through the Christian community and validated by personal Christian experience, it cannot stop there. Indeed, it must carry with it from the start the use of certain general presuppositions of knowledge when it makes a critical inquiry, though the Christian experience out of which it stems may take place without them. While these presuppositions interlock with one another, I shall state them one by one.

a. *The primary criterion of truth is the coherence of all available evidence.* The use of the coherence criterion is the appeal to systematic consistency—inner freedom from self-contradiction and consistency with all available and relevant data.[12] We use it every day in the attempt to distinguish what is true. If a person tells a story to account for his actions and there is any reason to suspect the truth of what he is saying—whether a mother is trying to teach her child to

---

[12] The best treatment of the meaning and indispensability of the coherence criterion is in Edgar S. Brightman's *An Introduction to Philosophy,* chap. ii. See also L. Harold DeWolf, *A Theology of the Living Church,* chap. ii.

tell the truth or a court trying a man for murder—the first thing one looks for is signs of his contradicting himself. When new evidence appears which is inconsistent with earlier explanations or assumptions—even apparently trivial but crucial bits of evidence such as something dropped on the scene of the event—suspicions are confirmed or new hypotheses formed. It is by this essential though often unconscious process of trying to eliminate contradictions and get greater coherence and consistency in conclusions that the daily processes of truth-seeking are guided.

It is by an elaboration of this method that all inductive science proceeds. Empirical verification requires sensory observation, either under controlled conditions in experiments or in the isolation of factors to be looked at where experimentation is impossible, often with statistical enumeration of instances. But what is presented to the senses or registered mathematically when a count is made is never the last word. Rational inferences must be drawn, and this drawing of inferences requires the use of the coherence criterion. Only so can extraneous factors be eliminated and inclusive, conclusive generalizations be accurately arrived at.

It is sometimes contended that philosophical method utilizes other "ways of knowing" than the coherence criterion, notably sense experience, the pragmatic test of consequences, and intuition. In particular, "existential" philosophy, with its stress on the emotional and volitional aspects of existence, is skeptical of coherence as too barren and abstract. It is true that through all these various channels the data with which philosophy deals must come. We must look at the world and see what it presents to our gaze, both with our physical senses and with the moral, spiritual, or aesthetic vision which may more properly be called not sight but insight. The consequences which follow from events, whether these are physical events or the acts and ideas of persons, cannot be disregarded. The philosophy of today is permeated with the concept of process, and process involves both the consequences of events and the dynamic character of the event itself. Reason is not the only aspect of human existence, or its major drive toward action. But when all this has been said, it still remains true that in the welter of data which come to the human mind through many channels, the only way to sift the real from the illusory, and thus to arrive at valid knowledge, is to continue the search for an inclusive consistency.

A prejudice against coherence is in effect a renunciation of reason, for reason is the attempt to put ideas together with self-consistency and logical coherence. One may surrender the idealistic metaphysical systems which have been built on the assumption that the universe as a whole is a Rational Mind, but one cannot do so on philosophical grounds without using the processes of rationality, and hence of coherence, in the inquiry which leads to this conclusion.

But what of coherence in theology? Must not reason give way to faith? And does not this imply that not coherence, but paradox, is the prime theological method?

An affirmative answer is often given by neo-orthodox theologians, who charge liberal theology with being both too rationalistic and too dependent on the methods and the metaphysics of the now generally discredited Hegelian idealism. But before admitting this charge some distinctions are in order.

I have said, and must say repeatedly, that theology takes its start from the inherited faith of the Christian community. This faith is not in its entirety rationally or coherently grounded. Yet when one starts to theologize, his primary function is to apply the test of reason, and hence of coherence, to what this faith affirms. In this quest he finds many elements which may be termed ambivalent, or polar, or paradoxical—in simple words, two-sided. Among these are such basic matters as the transcendence and the immanence of God,

44

the divine and human natures of Christ, the freedom and the finiteness of the human spirit. To affirm one of these without the other is to leave out something true and vitally important. The paradoxical relationship must be affirmed.

Does this exclude coherence? By no means, if coherence is conceived broadly enough to include anything for which there are sufficient grounds to justify belief. It excludes a superficial or premature systematization. The search for comprehensive consistency requires the recognition of the fact of paradox (better termed polarity) as part of the data.[13] When theologians, as they sometimes do, use reason to disparage the place of reason in Christian knowledge, they are demonstrating the necessity of the appeal to coherence even in the act of decrying it.[14]

With this as basic, we may now look more rapidly at certain other general presuppositions of knowledge which philosophy lends to theology.

b. *The discovery of knowledge is a function of our total experience, not of intellectual processes alone.* This recognition does justice to what is valid in pragmatism, or the existentialist approach, or intuitionism, or mysticism, or in general the claims of religious faith. It is in effect to say that what we have to deal with in the attempt to discover truth does not come by one route only. The materials—whether "raw materials" or refined—the substance, the data, of knowledge are as broad in their scope as all of human life and beyond that, of the totality of the universe. Our apprehension of these materials must be a dynamic process in which

[13] Cf. H. F. Rall, *Christianity: An Inquiry into Its Nature and Truth,* chap. iii, for an excellent treatment of the necessary place of polarity in the search for Christian knowledge.

[14] The use of reason by Karl Barth to disparage reason is no new phenomenon. In the sixteenth century Richard Hooker, speaking of the anti-rationalism of some of the English Puritans, wrote, "They never use reason so willingly as to disgrace reason." *The Laws of Ecclesiastical Polity,* Book III, viii, 4.

we have "knowledge by acquaintance," not merely "knowledge about." We have noted that a Christian theologian needs to be a Christian to see the faith from the inside; it is also true that too much of the "ivory tower" in a philosopher or scientist will not yield him the desired objective detachment, but instead sterility, narrowness of outlook, and neglect of essential data.

Such broadness of scope in regard to the materials of knowledge and the multiplicity of channels of apprehension in no sense contradicts what has just been said of coherence as the sole, essential criterion of truth. Whatever the channels by which our data come, the only way to determine whether they present real knowledge, and hence not illusion or emotional preference but truth, is to see whether they hang together with inner consistency and cohere with all other tested and trusted facts. Dreams, fancies, hopes, and fears are not to be scorned; neither are they to be accepted as giving knowledge unless they are coherent with a world beyond themselves.

c. *All knowledge except of formal relations is incomplete, yet much is dependable.* Only in the fields of mathematics and formal logic (and hence in the juggling of symbols in formal relations which characterizes symbolic logic) can assertions be made with finality. Yet this does not mean that there is no certainty short of such finality. A large body of factual and incontrovertible knowledge, such as that fire burns, water is wet, and an unsupported object will fall, is acquired by the normal child by the time he is two years old, and this body of knowledge (not mere speculation or assumption) continues to be enlarged as long as a mind has any capacity for growth and an environment to stimulate it. Nevertheless, no one ever knows all there is to know in any field, scientific, religious, or otherwise. The quest for knowledge requires always a "growing edge," and can only be made in a mood of humility and openness to what lies beyond.

46

In the meantime, we must live by our tentative conclusions. As Carneades put it in the second century B.C., "Probability is the guide of life." But such tentativeness and living by probabilities need not plunge us into skepticism. There is much that we can know with adequate certainty, even though there is always more to learn and further thinking to be done about the meaning of what we know.

d. *Truth is objective and stable, though our apprehension of it is subjective, partial, and variable.* This is another way of affirming the absoluteness of truth in spite of the relativity of human judgments, though "absolute" and "relative" are ambiguous terms and therefore often more confusing than illuminating. What is meant is not that there is no variableness in what we seek to make true statements about—it is certainly true that the sun shines one day and not the next. Any true description must provide for variation in what is described, whether one's self, his neighbor, his surroundings, or the state of the world. In fact, it is absolutely true that this is so. What is meant by the objectivity, stability, and therefore the absoluteness of truth is that what we are seeking to describe in any search for truth is something "out there," not subject to our whims, private fancies, or erroneous judgments. This is the case even if the object of inquiry is our own mental states; we cannot imagine or conjure them up at will if we would describe them truly.

Truth means the agreement of our ideas with reality. Our ideas, since we are finite human beings not endowed with omniscience, are bound in some respects to be faulty. Reality, however defective from the standpoint of what we might like it to be, remains objectively real, the stable point of reference in any judgment passed about it. A mountain remains a mountain even when obscured by clouds or dimly seen because of faulty vision. We must at the same time affirm the relativity of all human knowledge and reject an epistemological relativism that would deny the objectivity of truth.

e. *The human mind and the external world are organic to each other.* This does not mean that in a metaphysical sense, mind and nature are equally ultimate constituents. What we are discussing here is epistemology, not metaphysics, and to affirm their interrelatedness in the process of knowledge is not to affirm an ultimate dualism of substance or of causation. It is rather to say that they exist in such organic connection that we do not first begin with a mind and then leap across a chasm to something for the mind to work upon; in any mental state an external world—whatever the nature of that world—is always presupposed. Archbishop Temple's analysis of the "Cartesian Faux-Pas" is conclusive.[15] Descartes set a great deal of Western philosophy on the wrong track when, shut up in his stove and having nothing better to do,[16] he decided that he could doubt everything except the fact that he was doubting, and therefore came out with his *Cogito, ergo sum.* Actually he could not have been doing this doubting at all unless he had presupposed a world about which to be doubtful—even temporally and for such unusual purposes! From the moment that mental apprehension begins in infancy, when one thinks at all, he thinks in the context of a world objective to himself and shared by other human beings. Whatever our metaphysics, our epistemology must be grounded not in idealism or in rationalism but in realism.

f. *For any knowledge, certain presuppositions are necessary.* Reduced to a minimum, these are four: (1) the existence and dependability of the external world, (2) a common world of experience, (3) the trustworthiness of our mental powers, and (4) the interpretative activity of the human

---

[15] *Nature, Man and God,* chap. iii.

[16] "Finding no conversation to divert me, and having furthermore, by good fortune, no cares or passions to trouble me, I remained all day shut up alone in a stove, where I had full leisure to entertain my thoughts." *Discourse on Method,* Part II. (The stove was doubtless the chimney-seat of a spacious fireplace.)

mind. The first we have already discussed. The second has been hinted at, but requires a further word. Solipsism, the belief that one's self alone exists, is the *reductio ad absurdum* of a false epistemology and was never held by a sane mind. In spite of the existence of inner areas of isolation and of uniqueness in every individual, there could be no philosophy, science, religion, or any other enterprise of truth-seeking unless it were in some respects a corporate enterprise. The third must be affirmed, along with a humble recognition of our fallibility, if we are to believe that any truth whatever is attainable. Our intellectual integrity rests, not on a life-long "maybe," "perhaps," "possibly," "it might be so," but on the mingling of such qualifying phrases with the assurance of "This I have found to be true." And in any quest for truth, in the fourth place, the mind does some finding, and in the process puts something of itself upon what is found. The difference between a clear-seeing and clear-thinking mind and a muddy or clouded one lies not in the presence or absence of interpretation, which is inevitable in any case, but in the degree to which the interpreting is done objectively, inclusively, and hence coherently.

There is no philosophy, science, or religion without pre-suppositions. But presuppositions are essentially acts of faith! This is not to say that in all three fields these acts of faith are identical. It must be insisted, however, that there is no knowledge without initial elements of faith.

g. And finally, *values are facts*. What men prize, love, and live for is as much a part of existence as are sticks and stones, atoms and electrons. Of course, the fact that a man values something does not make the object of his longing either existent or inherently valuable, whether it be the peace of the world, the love of a maiden, or the touch of King Midas. It is the task of both ethics and religion to define true values and point the way to their attainment, and this is a large order in itself. What we are here concerned about is the fact that *truth* as well as goodness eludes us unless the whole range of man's existence, including his loves and loyalties, is taken into account.

It is clear that this is important to religion, for faith as commitment means valuing—believing in something or some Person enough to stake one's life on that conviction. But it is not in religion alone—it is in the total quest for truth—that values matter. To leave them out of account is to foredoom the quest to frustration or false conclusions through narrowness and foreshortening of vision.

I have tried in the last few pages to state the common requirements of a valid epistemology, whether in metaphysics, science, religion, or any other field. Any theology that is either philosophical or in a true sense biblical must carry these canons into its interpretation of the Christian faith. A doctrine of revelation can add something to these categories, as we shall see in chapter four; it cannot safely subtract from them. No apologetic can stand which disregards the conditions under which *all* truth-seeking must proceed.

CHAPTER III

Theology and Scientific Method

THE GENERAL PRESUPPOSITIONS OF KNOWLEDGE OUTLINED IN the previous chapter must go with us in all we undertake. There can be no valid pursuit of truth through any discipline without them. It is tempting to move immediately into the field of revelation and biblical theology to see how they apply, and thus how faith and reason can be co-ordinated. And there is nothing to prevent the reader from skipping this chapter if he desires to do so!

We must certainly, before we finish, give careful attention to the meaning of revelation, the canons of biblical interpretation, the validity of mystical experience and the witness of the Holy Spirit, and the uses and abuses of historic creeds. But to turn now to these studies would mean a bypassing of a major aspect of modern thought. Our age, for better, for worse—and, as we shall presently note, for better and for worse—is thoroughly steeped in scientific thinking. Christian theology can neither repudiate it, nor wholly embrace it, nor be indifferent to it. A crucial problem lies in how to come to terms with scientific method and at the same time to assert the rightful and distinctive claims of Christian faith.

1. *The meaning of science*

Perhaps we had better start as we did with reference to philosophy—with some definitions of terms. At the beginning of chapter 2 it was stated, "Science as a method means empirical inquiry aimed at the discovery of facts in any area of observable reality; particular sciences are specialized investigations and compilations of related data within chosen fields." Let us go on from there.

No science or group of sciences can be adequately defined without an adjective before the term. There are, we noted, certain normative sciences—logic, ethics, and aesthetics— which in the usual meaning of the word are not sciences at all, but branches of philosophy. The two major divisions of science as such are the descriptive and applied sciences. The definition just cited aims to say what the descriptive sciences are. Their object is to discover the facts in any given field and formulate from these discoveries the laws of structure and behavior—the great universalities of operation—in the field investigated. Where possible, these regularities are stated in mathematical equations.

The fields of scientific inquiry are in turn grouped as the natural sciences, such as physics, chemistry, and astronomy, where the precision of operation is so great that mathematics is not only useful but indispensable; the life sciences, where great regularities are observable but also individual varia- tions; and the social sciences, where common modes of be- havior are discoverable and statistical averages can be calcu- lated, but the variations in particular instances are so great that precise prediction is impossible and mathematical formulas have relatively little place. The tendency of some to regard biology and the sciences of human relations— psychology, sociology, and the like—all as natural sciences is a form of "reductionism" which views the field of investiga- tion in the way one would like for simplicity's sake to find it, not as it actually is.

In all these fields a large and ever-increasing body of knowledge has been accumulated. So impressive are these results that laboratories multiply in every institution of learning, and it is the mood of our age to regard scientific knowledge as real knowledge, and all other claims to knowl- edge as of dubious standing. In some areas, notably astronomy and biological evolution, the indisputable evidence of the descriptive sciences contradicts inherited Christian tradition, and theology must either revamp its claims or defy the sciences. In every area, the quest of science for regularities to be described through the formulation of laws casts doubt on the whole idea of miracle as the suspension or violation of natural law—and miracle is deeply imbedded in the Bible. It is obvious that the issue is joined in a way that cannot be evaded.

Liberal theology has for the most part come to terms with the descriptive sciences through its surrender of biblical infallibility, its stress on general revelation, and its tendency to view every scientific discovery as further knowledge of the processes by which the all-wise Creator works. But what of the applied sciences?

A phenomenal increase in the range of the applied sciences is the mark of a utilitarian, technological age. In spite of the doubtful value of the increase in millions of gadgets and all sorts of consumers' goods which are available today in the Western world, utility and technology ought not to be terms of disparagement. As physiology and anatomy are descriptive sciences, so medicine and surgery are applied sciences, and scientific healing has brought about an amazing extension of human life. Electrical development, synthetic chemistry, precision tooling, and the whole complex structure of present-day industrial production have opened up worlds undreamed of by our fathers. Barriers of space and time, though not wholly conquered, have been enormously reduced. Whether people today are happier than in the days of the Puritans and of the frontier is an open question; they are certainly physically healthier, more comfortable, more surrounded with things of beauty and with the tools for labor-saving and efficient action. All this is the product of applied science. In fact, it is a grim but suggestive thought that the two areas of greatest achievement in our time are scientific healing and scientific killing! Great medical discoveries and atomic and hydrogen bombs are running races with each other for the life of man upon the planet.

Ordinarily the applied sciences are not thought to present any particular problem to Christian theology. At a deeper level, however, the very life of religion is threatened by the idolatry of the worship of material goods and the putting of trust in scientific achievement rather than in God. And if the Christian religion should be "edged out" by the products of applied science, we shall have only memories left to theologize about.

The conflict between the Christian gospel and the worship of the products of the applied sciences belongs, for the most part, in the field of Christian ethics. It is relevant to homiletics, evangelism, and every effort to communicate the gospel. It is therefore tangent to Christian apologetics. But it is not central to our problem. The methods and assumptions of the descriptive sciences are. We must now examine these from the standpoint of how they relate to Christian theology.

2. Common elements and legitimate differences

Descriptive science and theology have certain points in common which, as in the case of philosophy, can cause mutual reinforcement or tension. The tension is not so inevitable as in the case of philosophy, but it always lurks in the offing.

First, both science and theology deal with one world. They deal with it from a different perspective, for science seeks to describe it and theology to state its ultimate source, meaning, and goal. Nevertheless, it is the same world, and any claim that certain things about it may be true according to science and not true according to Christian faith gets shipwrecked on this fact. Any "doctrine of the double truth"—whether held by the medieval Catholic church or by a puzzled university student of today who tries to hang on at the same time to the findings of biological evolution and to a six-day creation as taught back home in Sunday school—is bound to be wrenched apart when one's mind begins to work. Not a few human tragedies, wholly preventable with a wiser course, have stemmed from failure to grasp this fact.

It is often said that science deals with the phenomenal, and philosophy and theology with the noumenal or metaphysical, aspects of existence. This distinction, made famous by Immanuel Kant and deeply imbedded in the idealistic tradition, is of doubtful validity or usefulness. It is true that the terrain of science is the experienced world, which may be called the world of phenomena if one so desires. It is not true, on the other hand, that either philosophy or theology can leave this world to science and find its own standing ground elsewhere. The world we live in, composed of inanimate nature, organic living things, and human beings, is a real world—not the only world, according to Christian faith, but a very real one in the midst of which our lives are set. Our theology, like our science, must reckon with it, or be off center.[1]

And in the second place, both science and theology are in pursuit of truth, and truth, like the world in which it is sought, is one. This is not to say that either discipline can give us the *whole* truth. Each has its appropriate mode of approach, and there ought to be *entente cordiale* as each admits that it does not have, and cannot get, the whole truth. Nevertheless, the enterprise of each, though fragmentary, is a legitimate quest for truth; and at points where they intersect, there can be no contradiction between them.

Let us illustrate this, both whimsically and in more formal language. George Orwell in his *1984*—itself a picture of what

[1] An illustration of failure to reckon with the identity of the worlds with which science and theology deals is found in Karl Heim's *Christian Faith and Natural Science,* where it is contended that knowledge in the two realms is disparate because they exist in different *spaces,* or dimensions of being.

science may do to destroy us if not co-ordinated with moral values—has popularized the phrase "double think." The land of doublethink is a country where the Ministry of Joy looks after prisons and the Ministry of Peace looks after the maintenance of a chronic state of war! The application to be drawn is that scientific method and religious knowledge cannot be in a state of "double think" if both are searching for the truth. And since science by its dependence on natural law presupposes the universal *logos* evident in nature and Christian faith centers in the concrete *Logos* revealed historically in Jesus Christ, there cannot here be contradiction either. There can be differences in approach; there cannot be contradiction in results. As Paul Tillich puts it:

> The Christian claim that the *logos* who has become concrete in Jesus as the Christ is at the same time the universal *logos* includes the claim that wherever the *logos* is at work it agrees with the Christian message. No philosophy which is obedient to the universal *logos* can contradict the concrete *logos,* the Logos "who became flesh." [2]

All that has been said thus far about the correlations of faith and reason and the need of a dynamic synthesis bears upon this point.

And in the third place, in spite of differences there is a meeting point in method. The major note in scientific method is the verification of hypotheses—the mental apprehension of a possible explanation of observed phenomena and then the patient testing of this "guess" by further observation, experimentation under controlled conditions, isolation of extraneous elements, the use of appropriate tools of measurement, and the examination of sufficient instances to make certain that an apparent correlation between hypothesis and phenomenon is no accidental convergence. Sometimes such

[2] *Systematic Theology,* I, 28.

investigations cost many millions of dollars, as in the great laboratories for atomic research which finally split the atom and ushered in a new age of potential global destruction or economic power; sometimes they cost years of patient effort under discouraging conditions, as in Marie and Pierre Curie's discovery of radium. In any case, they involve faith in the possibility of discovery and faithful, persistent effort to reach conclusions which can then be used as the basis of fresh discoveries.

Note that in the last sentence I referred to the scientist's "faith" and "faithfulness." At this point there is more than an accidental conjunction with terms native to religion. *The Christian life is itself an endless testing of the hypothesis of God accepted in faith and then faithfully pursued.* I do not mean to imply that there is the same conscious devising of conditions for experiment or the same search for mathematical precision. The mood of scientific inquiry is essentially one of search; that of Christian faith living by great assurances. Nevertheless, both procedures assume that there is truth to be discovered, make a bold venture of the enlightened imagination, and then test it faithfully by the method of "try it and see."

But what of the differences between science and theology? For differences there are, which when recognized are no barrier to friendly relations.

It is commonly said that science deals with facts and religion with values. This is true, but it is not the whole truth, and put thus bluntly it is inaccurate. Science is the search for facts, to be correlated as laws, and a scientist qua scientist is not obligated to be concerned with any value except that of truth. Religion means apprehension of values through faith and living commitment to the purposes and power of God. But religion cannot rest on values unless these values are believed also to rest on "facts" in the sense of true convictions about God, man, and the world. When one reaches the point

of believing that his object of worship is not a factual reality
—that is, a Being objectively existing—he no longer worships.
This is not to say that God must exist in the same way that
stars, atoms, living cells, or other human beings exist, but
unless He (or It) is a reality about whom it is possible to
make true affirmations, religious experience has no standing
ground.[3]

Two common errors emerge from failure to recognize
these agreements within difference. One is a tendency to
chide science for its moral neutrality—its creation of bombs
that may destroy the human race or its attitude of detached
unconcern in analysis of precious human loves and loyalties.
A scientist, certainly, like any other man should have a conscience, but he ought not to be censured for the rigorous
pursuit of truth, which as a scientist he considers to be his
main business. The "opposite number" to this error is itself
a double-barreled one, for some regard religion wholly as
an attitude requiring no factual objective basis, while others
will have nothing to do with Christianity unless both the
power and the mercy of God can be proved by scientific
evidence.

A second important difference relates to the scope of inquiry. It is often said whimsically that a scientific expert is
"one who knows more and more about less and less." This is
literally true. The business of the scientist is exploration and
analysis in specialized fields—often very highly specialized
ones—and his success as a scientist depends upon the intensity
of such specialization. As a man, and as a philosopher of
science if he assays to be one, he must have a broader vista,
and the better he knows related fields, the more effective

[3] For this reason I cannot go along with Professor Tillich, who repeatedly asserts that "God does not exist." By this he does not intend to
affirm atheism, but the difference between God and every space-time
being that can be scientifically investigated. His deity is not *a* Being but
the Being, the Unconditioned Ground of all that exists. This difference
may be granted and still the existence of God affirmed.

his research in his chosen territory. But in one's capacity as a natural scientist he has no obligation to hold distinctive views upon politics, economics, art, domesticity, or religion. The theologian is equally absolved from knowing all that his scientific neighbor knows—but not absolved in the same way. He need not know the precise details of any of the specialized sciences, but he must have an inclusive view that relates them all to the ultimate Ground of Being. He may himself be a specialist in biblical interpretation or historical theology; he cannot as a systematic theologian surrender inclusiveness to specialization. At the point of seeking a synoptic, comprehensive vision rather than detailed analysis, the theologian stands with the philosopher rather than with the scientist.

A third difference has already been presupposed—and in it the scientist stands with the philosopher and the theologian is on the other side. This is the mood of objectivity and detachment with which scientific truth must be pursued, as over against the living commitment of the theologian. This statement can easily be misunderstood, as if the theologian had a right to inject his subjective prejudices into his conclusions and believe whatever he would like to believe! Many, in fact, do make this charge against theologians—and some deserve it. On my desk as I write are two interesting documents, one an advertisement of a book which by "many infallible proofs" professes to prove scientifically the verbal inerrancy of the Scriptures, another a vitriolic blast against me under the intriguing title of "The Voice of Apostate Religion." Dogmatism, from whatever angle it appears, exposes the proponents of religion to the charge of mongering their private preferences and antipathies, and what seems truth to one is apt to seem dogmatism to another. Nevertheless, the theologian cannot rightly do other than stand within the circle of the faith he seeks to understand and systematize. However rigorous his fidelity to scientific method in his study of the Bible or Christian history—and he ought to be rigorous if he attempts it at all—when he turns theologian, an attitude of uncommitted detachment misses the very thing that theology is about.

When these legitimate differences are accepted on both sides, then scientific method and religious experience—and beyond these, the philosophy of science and Christian theology—can get along very well together. Liberal theology has gone a long way toward making clear, and therefore acceptable, these agreements and differences. The tensions emerge (1) when either side gets dogmatic and attempts to pre-empt the field, or (2) when either side gets so supine, or unconscious of its own "natural rights," that it surrenders prematurely what is its rightful claim.

3. *Theology and science in mutual support*

At numerous points Christian theology and scientific method have rendered valuable service to each other. At others, disruptive tensions have emerged, as indicated in the preceding paragraph. Let us look now at both sides of the balance sheet, beginning for the sake of encouragement with the asset side of the ledger.

First, theology is greatly indebted to science for the stimulus to patient inquiry, for observation of the world as it is and not as we should like to have it, for elimination of superstition and slavish dependence on traditional belief. This is not to say that either science or theology can break with the past. What we have inherited, whether it is the accumulated scientific wisdom of the race which every child and most adults must take on the authority of others, or the "faith of our fathers, living still" which is the stuff of theology, ought to be treated with respect. Where it is vital to thought and life, it should be kept until there is reason to give it up, and surrendered only for something better. But when through patient search new light appears, the new light must be followed. The scientific method, being committed by its very existence to such a quest, has had more than a little influence on liberal Christian thought in purging it of error and thus planting the feet of Christians on firmer ground.

This discovery of new light is most evident in reference to the historical approach to the Bible. It is a favorite charge of the ultraconservative that liberals doubt or reject the Word of God, deny its great affirmations of faith, and then "pick and choose" such passages as they want to retain to support their heretical and emasculated opinions. Nothing could be much further from the actual situation. What scientific method in regard to textual, literary, and historical study has done is to shed light upon the great message of salvation which is the theme of the whole Bible, and in the light of knowledge of its comtemporary history and literary structure, to enable this light to shine more brightly than it possibly could in ignorance of these factors.[4]

Vitally important also to Christian scholars is the use of scientific method in the study of church history and historical theology. Such studies require, on the one hand, patient, accurate, unprejudiced delving into the documents and records of the past; on the other, wisdom in interpretation and, in particular, wisdom in discerning the interweaving of spiritual with mundane factors. To sift the permanent from the transitory—to see the hand of God working in the midst of political maneuvers whether of Church or of State, the interplay of genuine spiritual dedication with economic status and prestige in the emergence of new churches and the setting up and the deposing of ecclesiastical heads—requires clear vision. The "creeds of Christendom" did not just happen; they were born of struggle and the effort to

[4] My *Toward Understanding the Bible* (New York: Chas. Scribner's Sons, 1954) gives a brief survey for laymen of the principal factors in such a historical and literary study of the Bible, and attempts to show how such knowledge throws light on the great ideas of the Bible.

defend a faith that might not be accurately articulated but was too precious to surrender. The past gives us not merely "outworn tradition"; it gives us some of that, but it gives us also a great tradition which can only be understood and entered into by the fullest use of critical judgment and scientific method.

A second area in which theology owes much to science is the extension of the range of general revelation. The fact that "the heavens declare the glory of God" and that one has only to "consider the lilies of the field" to see evidences of the Father's care, is, of course, elemental and requires no scientific knowledge. Brother Lawrence, unversed in any science save the simple knowledge required for performing the duties of his kitchen, gives singular testimony that general revelation can also be saving revelation as he says of his conversion:

> That in the winter, seeing a tree stripped of its leaves, and considering that within a little time the leaves would be renewed, and after that the flowers and fruit appear, he received a high view of the providence and power of God, which has never since been effaced from his soul.[5]

It may be doubted that apart from a Christian context the sight of the tree would have brought about the saving of his soul and led him to that "practice of the presence of God" for which we are still today indebted to him. The point here is simply that even in the absence of scientific knowledge there can be general revelation of a high order, as Jesus' use of nature parables attests. Yet the more one knows of science, the more one sees of the majesty and mystery of the works of the Creator. Not only the beauty and the bounty, but also the intricacy and infinite orderliness of nature are eloquent of God.

[5] *Brother Lawrence: His Conversations and Letters on the Practice of the Presence of God.* Forward Movement Edition, p. 5.

It is most unfortunate that the long struggle over evolution versus six-day creation has torn so many minds asunder, and led not a few to think that they must decide between God and evolution. For the most part, this battle is over among thinking Christians, and settled not with an "either ... or" but by the concept of God working with long purposes through processes of evolution. Yet the struggle has not been all loss, for to many has come through biology and geology a greater God than before—infinitely greater in wisdom and creative power, and by analogy greater in love and mercy also. The cosmological argument for God, though it will not stand by itself to give all we need to know about God, has not been banished but given richer meaning through the wealth of modern scientific knowledge about God's world.

A third channel of service from science to religion belongs mainly in the fields of applied science and applied religion, but we may digress briefly to mention it. This is the vast amount of help which comes from scientific equipment in carrying and communicating the gospel and bringing the healing, serving ministry of Christ to those in need. People *did* tell others of Christ and minister in His name before there were any trains, automobiles, airplanes, telephones, printing presses, mimeograph machines, color film, movies, radio, or television. People healed before there was hospital equipment; taught before there were textbooks or universities; farmed before there was any scientific agriculture. Now that these things are among us, they ought to be put to the service of God for the enhancement of His glory and the furtherance of His Kingdom among men.

A particularly crucial field is one in which we have barely made a beginning—the bringing together of scientific psychotherapy with the Christian understanding of, and ministry to, sick souls. This area reaches into the depths of Christian theology, as such books as David Roberts' *Psychotherapy and a Christian View of Man* and Albert Outler's *Psycho-*

therapy and the Christian Message suggest. Encouraging beginnings have been made; much more needs to be done from both sides if the insights available from these two great sources of our knowledge of man are to yield mutual support.

In our time the debt of religious thinking to scientific thinking is more often acknowledged than the reverse. But this ought not to lead us to forget that theology was long regarded as the "queen of the sciences," and that the generative impulse of religion upon the cultures affected by it has caused it to be called "the mother of the arts." [6] The late Alfred North Whitehead, himself fully at home in science as well as in philosophy, continually stressed the mutuality of knowledge, and in *Science and the Modern World* stated that the modern scientific spirit with its confidence in the law of cause and effect is an outgrowth of the medieval faith in a rational God.

It must come from the medieval insistence on the rationality of God, conceived as with the personal energy of Jehovah and with the rationality of a Greek philosopher. . . . The faith in the possibility of science, generated antecedently to the development of modern scientific theory, is an unconscious derivative from medieval theology. [7]

Sir William Dampier in *A History of Science* gives numerous examples of this mutuality of knowledge, among which he traces nominalism from concern about the elements in the Eucharist to its emergence in the inductive method. [8] Francis Bacon, commonly regarded as the founder of modern scientific method, believed very strongly in the possibility of natural theology, and defined it as "that spark of knowledge of God which may be had by the light of nature and the

[6] W. E. Hocking, *The Meaning of God in Human Experience,* chap. ii.
[7] Pp. 18, 19.
[8] P. 87.

consideration of created things . . . *divine* in respect of its object, and *natural* in respect of its source of information." [9]

Quite apart from these important ideological historical connections, the Christian impulse to service by spreading the light of secular learning as well as that of the gospel has enormously undergirded the rise and dissemination of scientific knowledge. It is, of course, possible to point to numerous instances of the advance of science in the teeth of religious prejudice, as in the belief that epidemics were sent by the wrath of God and/or that with sufficient prayer, one could safely defy the laws of nature and come through unscathed. But when such charges are made, it does not do to forget that a vast system of schools and universities, to say nothing of hospitals and research foundations, owe their origin more to a Christian impulse than to any other factor. The relations of the Christian religion to science, both in theory and in practice, is a two-lane highway on which both can travel— and often have traveled to their mutual profit.

However, these relations have not always been pleasant or profitable. The natural question is, "Whose fault is it?"

4. *Theology and science in conflict*

We said earlier that disruptive tensions emerge when either party gets dogmatic and tries to occupy the entire field, or when either gets so supine that it is content to lose its own natural birthright. Let us see now how this has come to pass.

Scientific method, being the younger, lustier, and in many respects the bolder of these two disciplines, has not surrendered to theology, and is not likely to. Theology has sometimes surrendered to scientific method. Both have been dogmatic.

To begin with theology, its faults vary according to the kind of theology. In fact, from the standpoint of emotional

[9] C. C. J. Webb, *Studies in the History of Natural Theology*, p. 2. Italics his.

tension, the cleavages are often deeper between differing points of view in theology than between any of them and science.

Fundamentalist theology, when it becomes polemic, attacks those who listen to science at points where the literal infallibility of the Bible is in question, and contends that all such alleged knowledge is "science falsely so-called." It also has strange ways of twisting science to its own purpose, as in defending the virgin birth on the basis of parthenogenesis or figuring out a way in which the sun could have stood still for several hours over the vale of Ajalon. It illustrates the dogmatism of theology when it invades the field that rightly belongs to science.

Liberal theology has corrected this error but fallen into another. Not all, but too much, liberal preaching and writing in the first half of the twentieth century have done obeisance before science in a way that is not the best service to the Christian faith. Sometimes this has manifested itself in excessive deference to natural theology, often with the quoting of distinguished scientists to bolster the Christian cause. Very commonly, it has sucked the evangelical note out of Christian witness to leave only a rather commonplace and unexciting moralism as the residue. Among thoughtful scholars, pre-eminently Henry Nelson Wieman and his school of thought, liberalism has become religious naturalism in the attempt to ground religious knowledge wholly in scientific method. While this more extreme form of liberalism has not become current in the churches, liberalism's surrender to science at the point of a loss of the distinctive evangelical note in Christianity has been widespread. From this mood we are emerging, but we still have a distance to go.

Sensing the limitations in both these procedures, the new orthodoxy has tried to regain the authentic notes of the Reformation by a return to biblical theology without biblical literalism. As a whole this movement has been fruitful, perhaps most fruitful at the point of forcing liberalism to re-examine its foundations. While the most eminent living theologians, Barth, Brunner, and Niebuhr, have broken with liberalism, some very effective voices widely listened to in the churches—such men as John Baillie, Donald Baillie, Walter M. Horton, John Bennett, Nels Ferré, Henry P. Van Dusen, Robert L. Calhoun, Daniel Day Williams, and, in a class by himself, Paul Tillich—are concerned to preserve the truth in liberalism while correcting its shortcomings by a more biblical faith.

There are so many facets in the new orthodoxy that it is impossible to pass judgment on it in a paragraph.[10] Little can be said about it which applies to all its exponents. The point, however, in which it bears on our present discussion is its general tendency to be suspicious of natural theology, to look askance at both philosophy and science as approaches to Christian truth, and either to reject or greatly to depreciate general revelation. To the degree that it does this it erects new dogmatisms, less vulnerable because less obvious than the older biblical literalism, but still outside speaking distance with the scientific mind. The intellectual of today may be intrigued by it; he seldom understands it, or finds in it a resting place for his mind and soul.

This brief summary suggests three routes by which theology has allowed itself to get off the road where it ought to travel harmoniously with science. But what of the mistakes of science? These also may be looked at under three categories, though they have so many ramifications that no one should suppose that in actuality they can be neatly pigeon-holed. The philosophy of science is itself in transition, and its forms are not always so self-consistent as to be sharply distinguishable the one from the other. Nevertheless, holding in mind that scientific method per se is not necessarily at variance with Christian faith, we can discern three types

[10] More will be said about it in chapter 5.

of ideological structure in which it is. These we may term the materialistic, the positivistic, and the naturalistic.

The older scientific *materialism*—not a type of science, but of philosophy called into play for the service of science —declared physical nature to be the only reality. There were, of course, recognized to be observable differences among the forms physical nature took; some inanimate, some made up of living cells, some in such highly complex organizations of living cells as to constitute human beings. According to this view human persons, though to be regarded essentially as biological organisms of the mammalian type, have a sufficiently developed nervous system to possess an order of intelligence above that of any of the subhuman animals. What man calls spirit in himself is, however, to be viewed merely as a complex organization of living matter which takes individual form through the interplay of inherited biological equipment with its environment. Freedom of choice, and hence of moral or spiritual decision, is an illusion. Not only is there no immortality of the soul, but no soul exists to be either temporal or eternal. And if the human spirit, as essential being able to direct its destiny, is excluded from reality, still more obviously is the divine spirit. Belief in a personal God, or the living God of Christian faith, becomes a formerly useful superstition inherited from the lore of a bygone day.

Materialism in its cruder forms is no longer widely held. Physics, under the impact of the quantum theory and the theory of relativity, no longer makes matter the ultimate stuff of existence, and in psychology the behaviorism of a generation ago has been abandoned or greatly modified. Nevertheless, the residual inferences of such a view are still very current. It is customary to reject vigorously in America the Marxist "dialectical materialism," which traces all moral and cultural forces to economic factors, but the type of materialism (more often called by its exponents naturalism or realism) which denies any metaphysical reality or status to either the human or the divine spirit is common in both intellectual and plebeian circles.

It must be stressed that this is not an inherent or necessary accompaniment of the scientific method. Nevertheless, it thrives chiefly on the tendency of science to reductionism. In the desire to reduce every phenomenon to its simplest components and to bring everything within a comprehensive system of natural law, if possible to relations that can be mathematically stated, there is always a tendency to describe the higher categories of existence in terms of the lower.

Consequently the spiritual tends to be reduced to the psychological; the psychological tends to be reduced to the biological; the biological tends to be reduced to the chemical; the chemical tends to be reduced to physics; physics, many say, tends toward the mathematical; and then in some instances the whole tends to evaporate into some vague mysticism.[11]

It may be said as a rejoinder to the reductionistic view that it is the business of science to deal with what it finds, not to reduce it to something which for the sake of simplicity or all-inclusiveness it would like to find! Yet the tendency to make of man "nothing but" an animal organism and of God "nothing but" a projection of the human ego continues to assault Christian faith at it foundations.

The procedures of *positivistic empiricism* go in from a different angle but come out with some of the same conclusions. This is the limitation of scientific method to what can be discerned or inferred from a critical examination of sense experience, and the rejection of any other knowledge as being not really knowledge but supposition, preference, or fancy. In short, we can be "positive" of whatever science tells us through our senses, as these are greatly amplified

[11] Nels F. S. Ferré, *Faith and Reason*, p. 93.

through laboratory techniques; we cannot be sure of anything else. This is the epistemological correlate of a materialistic or naturalistic metaphysics. It leads, strictly speaking, to an agnostic rather than atheistic conclusion about God. By the limitations of this method there can be no scientific knowledge of God, and in the absence of any knowledge it is impossible either to affirm or to deny God's existence. However, for all practical purposes in the Christian life, a God unknown and unknowable is the same as no God.

The trouble with positivism does not lie essentially in the limitations it places on scientific method, though it may well be asked whether there is not also a legitimate empiricism which centers in the examination of moral, aesthetic, and religious experience as well as sense experience. Scientific method does not deal with ultimate questions, and hence is bound to be agnostic about God. The point where this procedure attacks Christian faith is the claim that this is the *only* road to knowledge.

The challenge to Christian faith by way of *naturalism* has been touched on in our mention of materialism, but merits further differentiation. Naturalism as it is now most commonly held expands the term "nature" to include human as well as physical nature, and does not hesitate to claim for human nature certain qualities not only of intelligence but also of moral and spiritual apprehension which are not to be reduced to biological functioning. It is not infrequently joined with a humanistic, and sometimes less consistently with a mystical, view of religion. John Dewey, the greatest naturalistic philosopher of our time, was greatly concerned with the increase of human values. Professor W. T. Stace, whose famous essay, "Man Against Darkness," [12] was generally viewed as an atheistic pronouncement, has since in his *Time and Eternity* set forth an essentially mystical approach to

[12] *The Atlantic Monthly*, Sept., 1948.

religion on the basis of a reaffirmation of naturalism for the temporal order, mystical illumination for the grasp of the eternal order. There is also a kind of pantheistic naturalism, such as was found in mathematical and logical form in Spinoza and now is more often advocated in aesthetic terms, which views all nature as being self-contained yet somehow suffused with a transcendent meaning. In a class of its own, as an attempt to form a bridge between the naturalism of John Dewey and historic Christian faith, is Professor Wieman's religious naturalism, which makes God an immanent process of growth in meaning and value—the Creative Good within all existence.

We cannot linger here to discuss these highly suggestive systems. There is space only to point out, as the chapter ends, what is common to them all and how this common element relates to Christian faith.

Wherever naturalism is found, it denies the existence of any supernature. It not only eliminates supernaturalism in the crude popular sense of credulous belief in ghosts, witches, angels, and demons, but it becomes naturalism by virtue of the fact that it limits reality to nature—not to physical nature only, but to the spatial-temporal order of observable reality. Thus it limits knowledge to scientific method, though it may conceive this broadly enough to cover ranges of human experience beyond the purely sensory. Naturalism may or may not affirm the existence of God, but if it does, it must do so by defining God as a form of human experience or as an immanent process creating values within the world of human and physical nature. A transcendent Creator, Judge, Redeemer, Father, or Lord of history naturalism cannot have if transcendence means an objectively existing deity, transcendent not only to the individual man and his society but to the world.

Yet this *is* the God that Christian faith affirms! The terms just noted, or at least the concepts they symbolize, are basic

71

to the faith of the Christian community. Without them, Christianity becomes something other than itself. In spite of naturalism's most earnest efforts to be a bearer of spiritual values, its presuppositions force it to stand at crucial points outside the orbit of Christian faith.

We must turn now to see what fruits are yielded by the approach through revelation and biblical theology. If this gives us what we have good reason to regard as truth, scientific method cannot contradict but must reinforce and validate it. Without a basis beyond itself scientific method is barren at the point of our greatest need, and leaves us with what Archbishop Temple has hauntingly called "the hunger of natural religion."

CHAPTER IV

Revelation, Faith, and Knowledge

In the first chapter i mentioned in a preliminary way the importance of revelation to Christian theology; in the second I passed it by to speak mainly about the relations of philosophy to theology; in the third we examined the elements of mutuality, legitimate difference, and conflict between theology and scientific method. Although incidental references to revelation have been necessary because the whole of Christian theology hangs together as one piece, it has seemed best to defer extended discussion until a frontal attack could be made on the question of the meaning and status of revelation. We must now look directly at the central issue of the problem of Christian knowledge, the relations between revelation and reason and the place of faith in the pursuit of knowledge.

1. *The meaning of revelation*

There is no simple, clear, universally agreed-upon definition of revelation. In fact, the "hot spot" of the problem as to the relations of revelation to reason lies in what revelation is understood to mean. We must therefore survey a number of ways of looking at the term.

The common denominator amongst various views of revelation is the assumption that God has disclosed something. Everybody except the extreme skeptic agrees that there is something in the way of knowledge for man to *discover*. (And even the most thoroughgoing skeptic believes he has discovered skepticism to be true!) However, when the emphasis is not on man's discovery but on the *disclosure* by deity of what is to be accepted by the human mind, this is revelation. This idea of divine disclosure we shall take as a preliminary and incomplete definition as we note what is done with it by various points of view.

a. *Revelation as religious irrationalism.* What does revelation mean to philosophy? In general, nothing. Philosophers do not commonly use the term unless they wish to distinguish their position from one which professes to rest on revelation. When one's approach is centered in the analysis of observable phenomena and the rational deduction of meaning therefrom, revelation looks like an extraneous element—something thrust in to bolster a body of traditional beliefs and muddy the waters of empirical inquiry and rational inference. This is true not only when it is claimed that revelation comes through such extraordinary channels as visions, auditions, dreams, and the casting of lots, but in other forms as well. That there is a general "givenness" in all experience the philosopher readily grants, but unless this is termed revelation, as it usually is not, revelation belongs outside the sweep of the philosopher's inquiry. In this the scientist qua scientist agrees with him, although since it is not the scientist's function to make judgments about ultimate sources and meanings, he is somewhat more inclined than the philosopher to say that the data with which he deals is a revelation of the handiwork of the Creator.

To reject revelation as an approach to the knowledge of God does not of necessity rule out religion. One may still believe in God on the basis of natural theology, particularly if it takes the deistic form of assuming that the ordered unity of nature requires the inference of a Supreme Being outside it as its source. The rejection of revelation is often linked with a humanistic type of faith, as in Julian Huxley's *Religion Without Revelation*. What it does is to declare that the idea of God's disclosing anything to man is an irrational concept. Thus, it must either be rejected outright or seen for what it is—an irrational assumption which cannot be brought into any organic relationship with reason.

b. *Revelation as objective source of religious experience.* Philosophers of religion not infrequently hold a view of revelation which is intermediate between the rejection of revelation and its assertion in the form usually held in the Hebrew-Christian tradition. This view centers not only in the givenness of the entire external world, but in particular in the fact that wherever there is religion, the claims of deity to worship and obedience always present themselves as coming from an objective source. The moment one tries to pray to himself, his mood is no longer prayer. One may unite with others both in prayer and in moral activity, but when this is conceived as social conformity or even solely as social service, it ceases to be religion. Not the Christian religion only, but every other religion assumes a Beyond from which the worshiper receives his inspiration and his moral and spiritual directives. Sometimes this Beyond, or Other, is conceived as speaking with special meaning and potency to an individual who then becomes a channel for the transmission of such insights to others, as in Gautama the Buddha, the Old Testament prophets, Jesus, Mohammed, Joseph Smith, Mary Baker Eddy, the Pope when he speaks ex cathedra. But whatever its form, wherever there is religion, the knowledge of this Other is a two-way process in which there is believed to be not only discovery by man but disclosure by the divine. This objective note in religious experience may be termed revelation.

Nothing is more obvious as one studies the various forms of religion than the disparity of revelation claims, even when all are thought by the adherents of these variant faiths to be received from an objective divine source. Such a view of revelation cannot, therefore, on philosophical grounds be substantiated as the communication of a body of true ideas.

The subjective certainty of religious persons that they have received divine revelations neither proves nor disproves their authentic character, and the validity of these claims must be settled rationally by the coherence of evidence in the total situation.

This phenomenological view of revelation moves, therefore, in one or the other of two directions. It either merges with the first view, dismissing the subjective certainty attached to revelation as an irrational assumption, or it passes over into a dynamic concept—to be described presently—in which it is not *truth* from God but the *purpose and power* of God that is objectively given in religious experience.[1]

c. *Revelation as divinely imparted truth.* A third view is so deeply imbedded in the Christian tradition that it is what is most commonly meant when the term "revelation" is used. In fact, we might have started here, had it not been desirable to see first what philosophers do with the idea. This is the view that God imparts certain items of knowledge, through channels of His own choosing, whether through chosen individuals, the Bible, or the creeds of the Church. These disclosures are truths to be accepted on faith, which we should not otherwise have but which we can be sure of beyond any question because God has disclosed them. Sometimes these divinely imparted truths take the form of full-fledged theological doctrines, such as the Incarnation or the Trinity; sometimes they are more fragmentary and particularized, such as the answer to some baffling personal problem that an individual may have. The common focus is that God tells us some things which, accepted on faith, give assured knowledge. This view of revelation was held with minor variations from the earliest centuries of the Christian era to the nineteeth, received its fullest formulation by Thomas

---

[1] Edgar S. Brightman in *A Philosophy of Religion,* pp. 172-78, gives an excellent presentation of this position from the second of these angles.

Aquinas, and is still found extensively in both Catholic and Protestant thought.[2]

The idea of revelation as divinely imparted truth to be accepted on faith seems to those who hold it simple and clear, and lacking in all the subtleties that confuse other views. It makes a place also for knowledge of many things which do not require such revelation. We can know some things, not only about nature but about God, by "natural knowledge," and others only by a special act in which God imparts knowledge and we receive it by faith. John Baillie remarks, with an arresting hyperbole, that up to the nineteenth century any child could have told you what revelation meant!

He would have explained to you that at creation God had endowed man with the power of reason, and that by the 'unaided' exercise of this reason man had been able to find out some things about God; but that, at a later time, God had added to the knowledge thus at man's disposal by communicating to him certain further information which he could not possibly have found out for himself.[3]

Although this view in its main outlines has been the common heritage of both Roman Catholic and conservative Protestant thought, certain differences in application may well be pointed out.

In the Thomistic view, reason has a very large place, not only to give us natural knowledge of God's existence through His works, but in convincing us of the authenticity of the revelation of God contained in the Scriptures. "Sacred doctrine also makes use of human reason." [4] Thomas put so clearly both the possibilities and the limitations of a natural knowledge of God that we shall do well to quote him:

[2] The term "Catholic" is here used advisedly to designate both Roman Catholic and Eastern Orthodox thought, though limits of space forbid any detailed consideration of the latter.

[3] *Our Knowledge of God,* pp. 35-36.

[4] *Summa Theologica,* I, Ques, 1, art. viii.

77

Our natural knowledge takes its beginning from sense. Hence our natural knowledge can reach as far as it can be led by the things of sense. But, starting from sensible things, our intellect cannot reach so far as to see the divine essence; because sensible things, which are created by God, are not equal to the power of God which is their Cause. Hence from the knowledge of sensible things the whole power of God cannot be known; from which it follows that His essence cannot be seen. But because they are His effects and dependent on Him as their Cause, we can be led from them so far as to know that God exists, and to know concerning Him those things which must necessarily appertain to Him in virtue of His being the first Cause of all things, exceeding all that He has caused.[5]

Beyond this knowledge of God through the things of sense lies, according to Aquinas, a realm in which further knowledge is disclosed to the believer through faith. Reason in this area neither contradicts nor supplants faith but supports it. In this realm there is a progression of faith, understanding, and vision in which faith is available to all, understanding to those who reflect upon it, and vision to those who in the next life will see God face to face though in the present this is granted only to the favored few.

Thus we have a majestic synthesis of faith and reason. Revelation is of divine grace, apprehended through faith, but reason has its place both before and in conjunction with what is given to faith. Why, then, did the Roman Catholic Church become so authoritarian? For various reasons, but basically from the twofold character of faith. Faith is not wholly a matter of the intellect—acceptance of truths about God as a supplement to natural knowledge; it is also a matter of the will, and hence of the believer's temporal and external salvation. It is a supernatural virtue infused by divine grace. This virtue comes to the believer not through reason or natural knowledge, but through the sacraments of the

[5] *Ibid.*, I, Ques. 12, art. xii.

Church. Hence, finally, faith imparted by God through the Church is the believer's authority for knowledge, as well as for salvation, in those spheres which lie beyond the realms of sense.

This Thomistic view, too briefly summarized, held in it enormous possibilities. On the one hand, it opened the way for a theistic interpretation of nature not at variance with the claims of philosophy or of science. Medieval philosophy was a great and reasoned system of unified belief with God as its keystone and center. But on the other hand, beyond the world of observable phenomena, or "things of sense," it made the final authority an *ab extra* revelation to be discerned by faith from the Scriptures as interpreted by the Church.

The Reformation dropped out from the Thomistic system the authority of both reason and the Church in divine matters, and left as supreme the authority of the Scriptures interpreted by the Holy Spirit. While Calvin has a chapter in the *Institutes* on "Rational Proofs to Establish the Belief of the Scripture," [6] and the Reformation leaders, like their present-day successors, freely used reason to demolish the claims of reason, the primary appeal was to the revealed Word of God in Scripture. This came in practice to mean generally among Protestants the Bible, literally interpreted, with only such sectarian and "enthusiastic" groups as the Quakers and Methodists making much of the authority of the Holy Spirit in interpreting the Word.[7]

The Westminster Confession of Faith may well serve as an example of this conception of revelation as divinely revealed, and hence authoritative, Scripture. It states that "it pleased the Lord, at sundry times, and in divers manners, to reveal himself and to declare his will unto his Church; and after-

[6] I, 8.

[7] Cf. Ronald Knox, *Enthusiasm*, for an excellent study of the groups throughout the history of the Church who have relied mainly on the inner voice of the Holy Spirit as their authority for faith and action.

wards, for the better preserving and propagating of the truth
. . . to commit the same wholly unto writing." Furthermore,
"The Old Testament in Hebrew, . . . and the New Testament in Greek, . . . being immediately inspired by God, and
by his singular care and providence kept pure in all ages, are
therefore authentical." [8] This view is, of course, not held
today by all Presbyterians, nor is it the exclusive property of
those in the Calvinist tradition. It is the common view of
those conservative Protestants who hold to the verbal inspiration and literal infallibility of the Bible, and who have called
themselves fundamentalists because they believe that only
on this basis can the fundamentals of divinely revealed truth
be preserved.

What we have been considering, whether in its Roman
Catholic or Protestant forms, clearly subordinates reason to
revelation. Reason may be freely used to substantiate faith;
it may not be used as a counter-authority.

The difficulty of meeting this conception of revelation with
argument is evident, for by its inherent structure it is im-
pervious to logical rebuttal. Hence, it is bound to seem
dogmatic to one who does not hold it. One who holds it
may or may not be dogmatic in the sense of being bigoted and
regarding all who disagree with him as sunk in error. The
more significant fact is that, however urbane and generous
one's personal outlook, to hold this view is to assume that
it is in the nature of revealed Christian truth to seem un-
persuasive to those who do not accept by faith. At this point
not only does apologetic become difficult through the erection
of barriers to communication, but discussion on rational
grounds becomes futile because it does not touch the issue.

This initial predisposition to discredit reason if it assails
the claims of faith has long tended to make the philosophical
or scientific type of mind suspicious of revelation in this

---

[8] I, 1, 8. I have quoted it in the excerpted form used by John Baillie in
Our Knowledge of God, p. 37.

sense. To this wariness has been added, in the nineteenth and twentieth centuries, a new outlook upon the Scriptures. The historical approach to the Bible, calling for an examination of historical backgrounds, literary forms, and the recognition of "situation-conditioned" elements from the surrounding cultures and the immediate circumstances in which the writings were produced, make it impossible for one who understands its structure to hold any longer to a doctrine of its literal infallibility. As the supreme book of living faith its place is unassailed; as a basis for dogmatic faith it no longer has the simple authenticity it was once thought to possess.

These considerations meet in the fact that the idea of revelation as divinely imparted truth does not of itself give us what we most need: namely, a living encounter with God and a living assurance of His presence. Dogmas may be believed without question, and the Christian life still be sterile. Dogmatic belief may be joined with richness of Christian life and devotion; it may also be joined with a perfunctory acquiescence in what is held to be revealed truth, and a most unloving spirit. The trouble is that such a view of revelation with all its profession of dependence on faith rather than reason, is too intellectualistic. My late professor Edgar S. Brightman was fond of quoting the word of his professor Wilhelm Herrmann, "Orthodoxy is too rationalistic." [9]

4. *Revelation as God's self-disclosure to the receptive spirit.* Hence there has emerged a doctrine of revelation which is a relatively recent understanding of the term, though what it stands for is ageless. This is the view that God does not disclose *truths,* as items of knowledge; rather, He imparts *Himself.* To the man of faith God comes as grace and power, as living Presence, and from the transformation of life in this personal encounter convictions emerge which,

[9] Quoted also in *A Philosophy of Religion,* p. 176.

when tested critically and organized coherently, become the stuff of which theology is made. In such a critical examination and systematization reason has full play, but it would have nothing to theologize about save for the initial, living meeting-point of God and man through worship and obedience in faith.

There are important variations within this view, though they meet at the common center of holding theology to be the human rational product of a God-given vital encounter. A neo-orthodox form of it is the view held by Karl Barth and with modifications by Emil Brunner. We have already had occasion to state that Barth rejects all natural theology, and holds that "faithless reason" can have no knowledge of God. This is rooted in his view of the complete defacing of the image of God in man by the Fall, so that human reason is unable of itself to grasp any truth about divine things. Revelation comes therefore *senkrecht von oben* (perpendicularly from above) as the gift of God to the man redeemed through Christ, and only to him. Brunner, on the other hand, holds that the image is not wholly lost; that there is some possibility of the discovery of God through natural knowledge and hence through general revelation; but that this is not revelation of the only kind that really matters: namely, *saving* revelation. This comes only through faith in Christ. The complex structure of grounds and consequences with which philosophy, as natural reason, deals has been "broken into" by this divinely given, saving revelation, and as a consequence what seems a "scandal" to the man without Christian faith is to the Christian both the power and the wisdom of God.[10]

It is evident that this view of revelation is far removed

[10] Baillie, *op. cit.*, pp. 17-34, gives a clear summary and critique of these positions. For firsthand statements by Barth and Brunner see Barth's essay in *Revelation* (Baillie and Martin, eds.) and *The Doctrine of the Word of God;* Brunner's *Natur und Gnade, Revelation and Reason,* and *The Scandal of Christianity.*

from the naïve dogmatism of the biblical literalist. It accents faith as a personal relation with God and not solely as a matter of belief. This is the primary point in Brunner's *Wahrheit als Begegnung,* translated into English under the title *The Divine-Human Encounter.* Yet it may be questioned whether this does not rest back upon the assumption that God has imparted revealed truth which is to be apprehended only by faith. God discloses Himself through the Word, and the Word as it comes to us is imbedded not only in personal encounter but true doctrine as this is mediated through the Bible and the Church. The personal saving relation which alone is significant revelation is meaningless unless the Christology of the Christian Church is true. Its authenticity is both presupposed in the personal encounter and validated by it. Thus it appears that for Brunner also, though less evidently than for Barth, reason recedes before faith and provides no dependable ground for distinguishing between true revelation and fallacious claims.

What is needed is a synthesis of faith and reason in Christian experience. The best statement of this view, quoted so frequently in the past twenty years that it has virtually become a classic, is Archbishop Temple's in *Nature, Man and God.* So important did he regard this difference between revealed truth and the revelation of God in Christian experience that he repeatedly uses italics to emphasize his position. We find him saying, *"What is offered to man's apprehension in any specific Revelation is not truth concerning God but the living God Himself."* [11] And again in another passage, *"There is no such thing as revealed truth. There are truths of revelation, that is to say, propositions which express the results of correct thinking concerning revelation; but they are not themselves directly revealed."* [12] The Archbishop believed tremendously

[11] P. 322.
[12] *Ibid.,* p. 317.

in the importance of having such correct thinking done, but he did not think it ought ever to be assumed to be revelation per se.

How, then, does the personal encounter with God become revelatory? Temple again puts his finger on what is crucial, and common to the manifold forms of divine disclosure: "There is no imparting of truth as the intellect apprehends truth, but there is event and appreciation; and in the coincidence of these the revelation consists." [13] This is sharpened by the statement, *"He guides the process; He guides the minds of men; the interaction of the process and the minds which are alike guided by Him is the essence of Revelation."* [14]

The advantages of this view of revelation over the assumption of a body of divinely imparted truths are enormous. It makes a place for faith, for without the faith of personal experience—to the Christian, faith in God as apprehended in Christ—there would be no coincidence of event and appreciation whereby the revelation occurs. It makes a place for reason, for it is reason's function to give critical and careful attention to the theological deductions which may be drawn from this living encounter. It affirms the divine initiative as God seeks to impart Himself more fully to men; it not only leaves room for, but it accents and requires, the response of man's whole being.

This view of revelation brings together about a common center views which are in other respects very disparate. It can readily be seen to have affinities with the second view we have outlined, revelation as objective source of religious experience, but in a more Christ-centered context, since to the Christian the supreme event calling forth both appreciation and commitment is confrontation by God in Christ. Though at

[13] *Ibid.,* p. 314.
[14] *Ibid.,* p. 312.

variance with those elements in Thomism and the new orthodoxy which depreciate reason to exalt faith, it has a meeting ground in stressing the importance of faith as man's volitional and existential encounter with God. Daniel D. Williams in *What Present-Day Theologians Are Thinking*, after stating the general outlines of this view of revelation, remarks:

Barth, Tillich, the Whiteheadian school and the new Catholic personalism stress its importance. Richard Niebuhr's *The Meaning of Revelation* is an especially concise statement of this point. What it means is that Christian thought can be set free from the intolerable dogmatism which results from claiming that God's truth is identical with some human formulation of it. It gives freedom for critical re-examination of every Christian statement in the light of further experience, and in the light of a fresh encounter with the personal and historical act of God in Christ.[15]

This must not be taken to mean that all contemporary theologians, including those mentioned in the first part of the above quotation, accept this principle in just the same way, or draw the same deductions from it. There are still great variations as to the empirical nature of the encounter, its relations to a biblical, ecclesiastical, or social groundwork, its implications both for theology and for Christian living.

2. *General and special revelation*

I have thus far avoided discussion of a very central problem in Christian theology, the relations of general and special revelation. Since one cannot talk about everything at once, it has seemed better to establish first what we mean by revelation, and proceed from this standpoint. Adopting as our stance the dynamic or experience-centered view of reve-

[15] Pp. 64-65.

lation just outlined, we can now deal more briefly with this other major issue.

By general revelation is meant the channels by which God has made Himself known through nature—not physical nature only, but the common, openly observable aspects of human nature as well. The psalmist gave a perfect statement of general revelation when he wrote:

> The heavens are telling the glory of God;
>   and the firmament proclaims his handiwork.
> Day to day pours forth speech,
>   and night to night declares knowledge.
> There is no speech, nor are there words;
>   their voice is not heard;
> yet their voice goes out through all the earth,
>   and their words to the end of the world.
>   (Ps. 19:1-4, R.S.V.)

In similar mood the philosopher George Berkeley—who was also a bishop of the Anglican Church—wrote of nature as a "divine language," and said that "all the choir of heaven and furniture of earth" were telling us of God. Wherever evidences of the reality of God are seen—not only in the beauty, bounty, and orderliness of physical nature, but in human love and loyalty, the fact of conscience, the agelong struggle toward a better world, the sacrifice and self-giving even of common men—there we have evidences of general revelation. This is not to say that every item of human existence speaks of God, for there is much that is dark and evil, but rather, that throughout nature and human life there are openly accessible factors which are pointers toward deity and require God for their fullest explanation.

The belief in general revelation presents relatively few problems to one who is favorable to a religious viewpoint. The dogmatic atheist may still say that the Christian sees the world from a biased position, reading into the evidence what he wishes to find there. However, if one looks at the world as objectively as possible, he discovers that it "comes mixed," but with a preponderance of good over evil and of value or disvalue. This surplus of goodness, beauty, and ordered unity is unexplainable except as indices of the goodness and power of the Creator.

It is not our purpose here to canvass in detail these evidences of the existence and nature of God. Our inquiry in this book is the methodology of Christian knowledge, not its content, and these evidences have repeatedly been presented and evaluated elsewhere.[16] It is enough to point out here that the fact of general revelation is not usually questioned by one who believes in revelation at all. While we have noted that Karl Barth and his school of thought deny the existence of any revelation except that through Christ, general revelation is for the most part accepted by theologians of otherwise differing views.[17] It is also a meeting point between theology and a religious interpretation of science, for while science as such does not attempt to pass judgment on the existence of God, every scientific discovery gives new evidence to validate the word of the psalmist:

> O Lord, our Lord,
>   how majestic is thy name in all the earth!
>   (Ps. 8:1)

The real point at issue is not general, but special, revelation. What then is special revelation? And in what form, if at all, can it be accepted?

Special revelation, like the term "revelation" as a whole,

[16] I have presented these evidences in my *Conflicts in Religious Thought*, chap. vi; *Understanding the Christian Faith*, ch. iv; *The Recovery of Ideals*, chaps. ix-xii; and *The Faith by Which the Church Lives*, chap. v.

[17] This is illustrated by the fact that the theologically conservative Moody Bible Institute in Chicago has issued a very beautiful and moving film on the Creation.

means different things to different people, and much discussion of this subject is confused by lack of precision in the
definition and use of terms. We shall begin by outlining
these meanings. It may mean (1) revelation through religious experience, Christian or otherwise, as distinguished
from experience in general; (2) revelation through particular individuals—the prophets, saints, and seers whom God
chooses as His special channels; (3) revelation to particular
individuals, who thus receive what is not accessible to all;
(4) revelation through special media outside the regular
order of nature, which are therefore regarded as miracles;
(5) a unique revelation in Jesus Christ; or (6) revelation
through Christ alone to Christians only.

To these may be added a seventh, inclusive of a basic
note in all these but not identical with any: namely, the
impartation by a personal God to individual persons of
meaning, values, purposes, and a sense of His divine Presence. What one receives in such a living encounter supple-
ments but does not contradict what is presented through
general revelation, and it adds a new "glow" and a new
dynamism to all of it. Again Archbishop Temple says it for
us: "The evidence of God's special activity is indeed not to
be found in what baffles the intelligence, but rather in power
active for such purposes as may reasonably be supposed
divine. Where power and mercy are combined, there is God
manifest." [18]

This last view of special revelation correlates with what I
have presented as the most satisfactory view of revelation as
a whole. What is "special" about it is not the imparting of
hidden information or the use of extraordinary channels, but
the vitality of the individual person's encounter with a
Personal God, one's living awareness of the Living God.
This encounter, however much it follows the paths in which

[18] *Op. cit.*, p. 323.

others before have walked, or whatever corporate elements may attend it, is always a particularized experience. Francis Thompson, himself redeemed by divine grace from such despair as seldom grips men, expressed it vividly in the words:

> Heaven . . .
> Must of as deep diversity
> In judgement as creation be.
> There is no expeditious road
> To pack and label men for God,
> And save them by the barrel-load.[19]

From this standpoint what may be said of the other meanings of the term? Of the first, that religious experience wherever religion is found is a channel by which God imparts such power and vision; but this is not to say that all religions are equally clear channels, or that what is channeled is of equal moral purity and power. Christianity stands preeminent in what it reveals of the nature and activity of God.

Of the second and third, it may be said that there is no barrier to supposing that God reveals himself more clearly and with greater potency *through* some persons and *to* some persons than others. What we cannot assume is that God arbitrarily or capriciously chooses His favorites. Since everything in the divine-human encounter is a Person-to-person relationship, special revelations are to be expected, even as every man has a special vocation. If the love of God is directed to individuals, so is His light. Yet as God does not love one of His children more than another but manifests this love increasingly to one who will receive it in humble joy, so do we ourselves open channels or set barriers to divine disclosure. It is entirely reasonable to suppose that to some, a clearer revelation comes because of greater spiritual sensitivity and faithful obedience. When the psalmist prayed:

---

[19] Epilogue to "A Judgment in Heaven." Quoted by Baillie, *op. cit.*, p. 97.

Open my eyes, that I may behold
wondrous things out of thy law
(Ps. 119:18),

or the familiar words:

Let the words of my mouth and the meditation of my heart
be acceptable in thy sight,
O Lord, my rock and my redeemer
(Ps. 19:14),

he stated with spiritual fervor and with complete accuracy the conditions by which special revelations of God's power and mercy may come to some persons and not to others. Then through such persons, as willing vehicles and unclogged channels, the grace and the light of God are mediated.

The questions of the miraculous in revelation and of the uniqueness of the revelation in Christ are basic issues which cannot be disposed of hastily. But since this chapter has already reached its proportionate dimensions, we can do no more here than to point the direction to be taken.

If what has been said this far is true, special revelation is always found within the sphere of general revelation, not outside it and not in contradiction to it. *"We affirm, then, that unless all existence is a medium of Revelation, no particular Revelation is possible. . . . But if all existence is a revelation of God, as it must be if He is the ground of its existence, and if the God thus revealed is personal, then there is more ground in reason for expecting particular revelations than for denying them."* [20]

The existence of particular revelations within the sphere of the general revelation of God in all existence does not answer for us, either affirmatively or negatively, the question of miracles. The answer reached will depend largely on one's understanding both of the Bible and of science. What must

[20] Temple, *op. cit.*, pp. 306-7.

be stressed is that in the original sense of miracle as something to be wondered at—God's "wonderful works"—every
revelation is a miracle. Yet revelation, whether general or
special, ought not to be supposed to center mainly in the
unusual or the spectacular. Whether one exclaims regarding
the wonderful works of God in nature:

> I praise thee, for thou art fearful and wonderful.
> Wonderful are thy works!
>
> (Ps. 139:14),

or is speechless before the miracle of grace: "Thanks be to
God for his inexpressible gift!" (II Cor. 9:15), what is revelatory is not a deviation from nature, but the divine disclosure
to receptive spirits of God's power and mercy in such a way
as to call forth the response of amazement, gratitude, and joy.

If every special revelation is found within, and not in
contradiction to, general revelation, this is true of the supreme revelation of God in Jesus Christ. The incarnation
took place within the stream of historic Judaism and in a
person who in many respects shared the common lot of our
humanity; otherwise there would have been no incarnation,
but only the phantom-humanity of Jesus that the docetists of
the early centuries heretically alleged. What is unique about
Jesus is the particularity of his revelation of God within the
structure of human, historical experience.

But is Jesus Christ our only revelation of God? The foregoing has suggested the answer. That Jesus Christ is the
supreme revelation of God, indispensable to right knowledge
of God as well as to the fullest redemption through God's
grace, is a basic tenet of Christian faith. But to say that in
him is found the *supreme,* or the *only adequate,* revelation
of God is not to say that in him is God's *only* revelation.
Both the uniqueness of the revelation in Christ and its common ground with other forms of divine manifestation are
admirably caught by the author of the Epistle to the Hebrews:

In many and various ways God spoke of old to our fathers by the prophets; but in these last days he has spoken to us by a Son, whom he appointed the heir of all things, through whom also he created the world. He reflects the glory of God and bears the very stamp of his nature, upholding the universe by his word of power (1:1-3).

Faith, as we must keep saying because it is so essential, is not primarily assent to a body of theological truths—even to so basic a truth as the incarnation of God in Christ; faith is living commitment, surrender of will, the yielding of life to be molded by a supreme loyalty. Men may argue about Christological doctrines in reference to Jesus Christ; there is no argument about his unique capacity to elicit love and loyalty. Twenty centuries of Christian history and many millions of transformed lives attest it. Far beyond all other revelations, unique in his power to remold individuals and even great social groups, he commands our faith; he "reflects the glory of God and bears the very stamp of his nature." Through him the revelation of God in the natural order becomes meaningful; apart from him the existence of any revelation is called in question.

3. Revelation and the general presuppositions of knowledge

It remains for us to tie together some things said at the end of the second chapter with what has been presented in this one. If what has here been set forth is accepted, this can be done briefly; if not, no extended analysis would be convincing.

I stated as the general presuppositions of all knowledge:

a. The primary criterion of truth is the coherence of all available evidence.

b. The discovery of knowledge is a function of our total experience, not of intellectual processes alone.

c. All knowledge except of formal relation is incomplete, yet much is dependable.

d. Truth is objective and stable, though our apprehension of it is subjective, partial, and variable.

e. The human mind and the external world are organic to each other.

f. For any knowledge, certain presuppositions are necessary: the existence and dependability of the external world, a common world of experience, the trustworthiness of our mental powers, and the interpretative activity of the mind.

g. Values are facts.

If revelation is to give us valid knowledge of God, how then is it related to these conditions of knowledge as a whole?

The abstract form in which these propositions are stated, following close upon the statement of God's supreme and wonderful self-disclosure in Jesus Christ, suggests sharply the contrast between the philosophical and the biblical route to our knowledge of God. Contrast there is, but not conflict, for if the truth about God is one structure of objective fact, there can be no ultimate conflict between them.

Let us now look at each of these propositions in terms of what I have been saying in this chapter about revelation.

a. Revelation does not give us, per se, a body of revealed truth. What it does give is an experience of God, mediated through the Christian community, which presents data to be examined by the canons of reason and the use of the coherence criterion. The result is theology.

b. A purely cognitive approach to theology omits essential data of the encounter of personal faith. It therefore falls into one or the other of two pitfalls: the rejection of revelation or the dogmatic acceptance of creedal and scriptural assertions of revealed truth.

c. We do not have full knowledge of God. We have an adequate revelation of God in Jesus Christ; yet even so we "see in a mirror dimly." The appropriate mood is one of lifelong search for truth in conjunction with humble reverence before the mysteries of God.

d. The truth *about God,* like all other truth, is truth *from God.* Since all truth is objectively grounded in the reality and rationality of the Supreme Mind, the truth we seek in theological analysis of Christian experience has objective validity. True revelation must, however, be distinguished from mere revelation-claims by the test of coherence.

e. The human mind and the external world are so organically related to each other as to yield the conclusion that the world has been "put together mindwise." This makes possible the discovery of God through nature and the media of general revelation.

f. In any pursuit of knowledge certain presuppositions, which are essentially acts of faith, must be taken as initial assumptions. All of these come into play in the apprehension and testing of revelation, plus the more intimate and total faith involved in personal commitment to God in Christ.

g. Such a personal encounter is derived from, expressed in, and directed toward values. Faith is loyalty in trust, "the assurance of things hoped for, the conviction of things not seen." Not only is it a fact that such values exist; they point beyond themselves to assured conclusions.

Thus it comes about that while it is true—and must ever remain true—that "the primary assurances of Religion are the ultimate questions of Philosophy," the gulf is not so wide that it cannot be spanned. God is one and truth is one, but there are many channels to the apprehension of His nature. As reason on a sublime scale is revelatory, so is revelation rational in the sense that what is apprehended in faith must be tested by reason. What is most needed in our time is a dynamic synthesis of faith and reason if God is to be truly known.

CHAPTER V

The Authority of the Bible

THE PRECEDING CHAPTER HAS ATTEMPTED TO CLARIFY AND
defend five affirmations which the author regards as basic
to the right apprehension of Christian knowledge: (1) that
revelation is not only a valid, but an indispensable, approach to Christian truth; (2) that such revelation is given,
not in the form of impregnable dogmas or their compila-
tion as a sacrosanct corpus of Christian doctrine, but as a
living encounter with the living God; (3) that the faith
necessary both for this encounter and for the fuller apprehension of its meaning in theological terms is by no
means divorced from reason; (4) that while Christian
experience can occur with a minimum of rational content,
there can be no valid theology without a dynamic synthesis
of faith and reason; and (5) that in this dynamic synthesis
the general presuppositions of all knowledge must not be
left behind, but that on the contrary, legitimate modes of
pursuit of Christian truth are fully consistent with these
general presuppositions and must be co-ordinated with
them.

We move now to an examination of what through the
centuries has been regarded as the sphere of revelation par
excellence—the Holy Scriptures as the Word of God.

1. *The resurgence of biblical theology*

One of the dominant notes of contemporary Christian
thought is the movement of biblical theology during the
past two decades into a position of centrality. While philosophical and biblical theology have always been present,

from the days of the Hellenizing of the gospel onward, neither one completely excluding the other, there have been swings and counterswings in their status. As the period of the Reformation stressed the Bible and the Enlightenment a rational approach to the Christian faith, the after-effects of which lasted well through the first quarter of the twentieth century, so now the current is reversed and philosophical theology is rejected or widely suspect. A clear index of this is that the writing and discussion that go on among top-ranking scholars of the ecumenical movement is wholly in a biblical context—not, to be sure, with full agreement as to the interpretation of what the Bible says about such moot themes as the nature of the Church, the Christian hope, or social action, but with great unanimity of appeal to the Bible as authority.

For this biblical resurgence there are a number of reasons, all of which are interrelated with such complexity that only the main strands can here be pointed out. First to be noted, though less influential than more basic ideological factors, is the social turbulence and loss of external supports caused by economic depression, war, and tyranny. Here the difference in situation between America and our fellow Christians in Europe comes sharply into focus. While there has been an upturn of *interest* in the Bible in the United States, as evidenced by the remarkable sale of the Revised Standard Version, the filming of numerous biblical movies, and the introduction of courses in the Bible into many college and university curriculums, it can hardly be said that to any significant degree the Bible is a primary *support*. Although American standards are shaped by a long biblical heritage, both our separation of Church and State and inadequate instruction in the churches have prevented any general knowledge of its content. Relatively few Americans —or so it may be guessed—think much about the Bible except as they expect to hear some reading from it in the

Sunday morning service, to which they listen with rather desultory interest.

On the contrary, Christians who have lived through persecution, tyranny, constant bombardment, the loss of material possessions and too often of their loved ones have found in the Bible great strength and undergirding support. At the Madras Conference of 1938 a young German delegate said to me, "We read our Bibles more than we used to. It is all we have—and it is all we need." As the war clouds broke into torrents of suffering, with imprisonment, destruction, and death on every hand, this testimony became the experience of thousands. When the war was over, it was only natural that Christians as they came together found their deepest bond of unity in the Bible and took it as their charter of Christian faith and action.

A second element in the resurgence of biblical authority stems from the extraordinary influence of three living theologians, Karl Barth, Emil Brunner, and Reinhold Niebuhr. All three are prolific writers and very dynamic persons who are everywhere listened to with respect, though not always with either agreement or understanding. The very process of objecting to their thought has been educative, as many a "chastened liberal" will gratefully admit if he is honest! Their writings are more widely read and generally known throughout the Christian world than were those of Luther or Calvin in their day,[1] and may become as classic.

In spite of wide differences among them, they have a common center. All three were trained in a liberal, historical approach to the Bible and in contrast with biblical literalism, have retained its essential pattern. They are poles removed from fundamentalism, though Barth in his writings

[1] This is due, of course, not simply to their intrinsic character, but to the wider dissemination of printed matter and the increase in numbers of those theologically trained in seminaries.

sometimes seems not to be. None of the three is a professional biblical scholar. All three repudiate philosophical theology as a primary approach to truth, and put in its place a kerygmatic biblical center. Their combined influence is incalculable in repudiating Christian rationalism and stressing the Reformation note of salvation of sinful men through faith in Christ as this faith is known through the Bible.

A third element in the resurgence of biblical theology is to be found in the inherent weakness of what preceded it. Current castigations of liberalism, by the great neo-orthodox theologians just mentioned as well as by many of lesser status, often seem to me unfair. There were few, if any, Christian leaders in the churches who denied the sinfulness of man and his need of saving help from God, or who believed in automatic progress, or who made God so immanent that there was no transcendent holiness in His nature. There were secular liberals and some humanist exponents of Christian ethics who did this. But this was never the liberalism of Washington Gladden, Walter Rauschenbusch, Borden P. Bowne, William Adams Brown, Albert C. Knudson, Harry Emerson Fosdick, Ernest Fremont Tittle, Harris Franklin Rall, Henry Sloane Coffin, or any of the other great liberal Christian leaders of the late nineteenth and first half of the twentieth centuries. What these men and thousands of ministers trained under their influence have done was to find God *both* in the Bible and in the world accessible to philosophy and science; to see man *both* as child of God, of infinite worth, and as sinner in need of individual and social salvation; to find God as Creator, Redeemer, and Father *both* above and beyond this world and within it in nature and the currents of human history.

Nevertheless, with all the great good that came out of this dual emphasis of liberalism, it had its weaknesses. These defects lay not so much in what it erroneously affirmed as in what it left unstressed. Concerned with the moral applications of the teachings of Jesus in a world full of man's inhumanity to man, it said too little about the saving Christ. Concerned to counteract both the other-worldliness and the crude apocalyptic expectations of an earlier period, it largely lost the eschatological note[2] and talked much about "building the Kingdom" here on earth. Concerned to heal the breach between religion and science, it sometimes capitulated too far at the point of miracle and providence, and left the impression that religious truth must take its orders from science. Concerned to show the presence of God in the spiritual and moral strivings of all persons, it stressed "religious" experience and "religious" education rather than what is distinctively Christian. As a result the Bible, though studied historically with better understanding than in the past, became one source among many leading to the knowledge of God. Biblical theology lost the distinctive place that it had held in the Reformation and was still holding in conservative Protestant thought.

These underemphases, always more characteristic of the lesser exponents of liberalism than of its great leaders, got it into trouble. The combination of a real distortion at crucial points and misunderstandings between liberals and conservatives led to the "modernism" so widely decried, feared, and hated by traditionalists.[3] Roman Catholicism under the recently sainted Pope Pius X so effectively quashed an incipient modernism in its ranks, led by Tyrrell and Loisy and encouraged by Baron von Hügel,

[2] For the most part, however, liberalism has retained the Christian hope of personal immortality, and its exponents regret that so little is made of this in current eschatological discussion.

[3] Two sermons by Dr. Fosdick, printed in *The Christian Century* and widely read, are both symbols and instruments in this struggle and mark the decisive stages in liberalism. The first is "Shall the Fundamentalists Win?" issue of June 8, 1922; the second is "Beyond Modernism," Dec. 4, 1935.

that it has not since then lifted its head. Protestant liberalism survived to grow in power until its primary affirmative notes are now accepted and taught in most of the seminaries of the land, undergirding the thought of even those neo-orthodox leaders who inveigh against it. Its negations and underemphases have during the past two decades undergone radical correction.

Thus it appears that a combination of social forces, dynamic and able leadership, and inherent ideological trends has contributed to the accenting of biblical above philosophical theology in our time. All these factors come to focus in the World Council of Churches, in which there has been a great cross-fertilization of thought among theological leaders. And, since the main stress of this movement centers in biblical rather than philosophical theology, it has now become practically axiomatic for both European and American theologians to find their primary standing ground within the Bible.

2. Contributions and limitations of alternative views

The main issue is not now *pro* or *con* biblical theology; that issue seems to have been answered with a decided *pro*. Yet the question still remains as to how to conceive biblical theology. There are wide differences as to how to discover and utilize the Bible's authority.

While pigeonholing is always dangerous, there seem to be four dominant approaches to the Bible in contemporary Protestantism. These are the conservative, the fundamentalist, the liberal, and the neo-orthodox positions. Three of these we have already had some occasion to look at in connection with the relation of theology to scientific method. It is customary to equate conservatism with fundamentalism, but I do not think this is quite accurate, either with regard to historical or contemporary forms. Conservatism stresses an evangelical piety based on the Bible, but does not usually take any particular stand for or against science, while fundamentalism does. There are other differences to be noted presently.

a. *Conservatism.* Conservatism in any field means adherence to the past, and hence reluctance to make radical changes lest something that ought to be conserved be lost. This is true in the field of religion also.

The Christian faith was born in living experience, then early became associated with the apostolic authenticity of Scripture. In practice this meant biblical literalism without critical analysis. Up to the time of the emergence of the historical method, which began in Europe in the nineteenth century but did not make much stir in America before the beginning of the twentieth, biblical theology rested on this basis. Without the tools by which consciously to make any other approach, it was assumed that "what the Bible says" is the Christian's final authority.

Implicitly, however, another criterion had been applied from the beginning: namely, appropriateness to the revelation of God in Christ. What became Scripture in the period when the New Testament canon was in process of formation was determined not alone by its supposed apostolic origin, but by the quality of its apostolic message—its witness to the saving work of God in Christ. Comparison with non-canonical Christian writings such as Ignatius' letters, the Epistle of Barnabas, and the Shepherd of Hermas bears out the soundness of the judgment that was reached. Thus it was possible for the author of Second Timothy to say: "All scripture is given by inspiration of God, and is profitable for doctrine, for reproof, for correction, for instruction in righteousness" (3:16, K.J.V) .[4]

But though "all scripture" was thus regarded as inspired, something had to be done about the parts that did not

[4] I quote the King James Version because it is in this form that it has been immensely influential for the past three and a half centuries.

fit into what the Christian through his total experience believed about the love of God, salvation through Christ, and the demands of Christian morality. Allegorization was one method, not infrequently carried to extremes to make the Old Testament in every detail foreshadow the New. A more common method, however, was to find a hidden spiritual meaning in every troublesome passage and to pass over as "divine mystery" those which did not readily yield such a meaning. Thus the Bible could be read with great spiritual enrichment to the Christian life without raising critical problems.

This, in general, was the stance of the Reformers, and it has continued to be the approach of the conservative mind to the present day. Literalism has not been renounced, but neither has it been consistently accepted. John Calvin saw that the Bible must be interpreted through the Holy Spirit, which in practice meant the voice of the Holy Spirit as John Calvin, and not Luther, Zwingli, or Melanchthon, heard it. Luther did not hesitate to discern in the Bible different levels of truth, as his reference to the book of James as "an epistle of straw" gives evidence; nevertheless, he found in the Bible the ultimate source of the Christian's knowledge of the saving grace of God.

Protestantism from the sixteenth century to the twentieth followed in general this path of conservative, Bible-centered orthodoxy. Many Protestants still follow it—not pretending to understand all of the Bible, not much troubled by critical questions, unaware of any method to follow except to take it as it stands and find its spiritual message.

The results of this procedure have been mixed, but on the whole productive of much spiritual stability. The religion of our founding fathers was thus grounded. Until a generation ago it was the main structure of Christian life and thought in the Protestant churches of both Europe and America, and in many places it still is. It has bred warmth and depth of evangelical faith, and within small-group relations, where the claims of the Christian conscience were recognized, a firm-textured morality. A very large number, probably most, of today's liberal and neo-orthodox leaders grew up in Christian homes of which this conservative, Bible-centered faith was the main support.

b. *Fundamentalism*. What we have just been describing ought to be distinguished from fundamentalism. It passes over into fundamentalism by stages not always clearly discernible, but its mood and spirit are different.

Fundamentalism is biblical literalism in fighting mood. Basically it is an attitude, not of simple evangelical piety rooted in the Bible, but of polemical defense of the verbal inspiration and hence the literal inerrancy of the Scriptures. Usually it is connected also with a single-track interpretation of the Apostles' Creed, with much stress on the virgin birth, a substitutionary atonement through the blood of Christ, the physical resurrection and ascension of Jesus, and his visible second coming. Belief in these items of faith, as well as in the literal inerrancy of the Bible, is made the mark of being a Christian. Anyone who thinks otherwise is attacked both as deceived and as a deceiver leading the faithful astray.

Fundamentalism is conservatism turned rationalistic. Often decrying the rationalism of the so-called modernists, it uses all the resources of reason to resist any reinterpretation of the Bible or creeds which might arise from a discovery of human factors in the processes by which the Bible or the creeds came into being.

What are the fundamentalists trying to preserve? It is easy for those under attack to assume that they are trying, sometimes without much Christian love, to preserve their own cherished prejudices. The issue, however, goes deeper. To the fundamentalist, revelation and all the most precious things revealed appear to be at stake. It is a case of the

Bible "letter for letter" or nothing. Evolution is resisted as contradicting Genesis because it seems to eliminate the authority of the Bible, and with it the Creator God. The virgin birth (usually with incredulous disregard of any adverse biblical evidence) is insisted upon because there seems no other way to preserve the unique divinity of the incarnate Lord. To question the blood atonement is to question Christ's redeeming work. To question the physical resurrection, and subsequent ascension through the clouds, of the body of Jesus is to deny that Easter has any foundation. Revivalism is advocated, the social gospel decried, because the redemption of every man through the new birth seems all important.

Yet the liberals and the neo-orthodox, as well as the fundamentalists, prize the Bible as the vehicle of God's revelation and believe in the Creator God; the divine, incarnate, redeeming Christ; His resurrection in victory over sin and death; our perennial need of personal redemption. Then why so far apart? And why not get together? Basically because of a radical rift over *how to understand the Bible*. For all, the Bible is authoritative; yet in such a different way that this has become the deepest cleavage in contemporary Christianity. It cuts across denominational lines, and in the churches is far more divisive than any issue of the ecumenical movement. Even a little *rapprochement* at this point, if it can be achieved without surrender of conviction, ought to be welcomed as great gain.

c. *Liberalism*. There is a kind of secular liberalism that emphasizes freedom, democracy, and the dignity of every man —often with little familiarity with the Bible, and no reliance upon it. This at some points, such as insistence on the elimination of social, racial, and economic injustice, is tangent to Christian faith; but it is not essentially Christian. It may even be openly atheistic. John Dewey stands as its foremost representative in modern times. It is primarily the product of Greek and Roman and Renaissance thought, set in a modern framework, rather than of the Christian faith. We are not concerned with it here because, although there are individual Christians who have this outlook,[5] it has not made much headway in Christian churches.

There is also, we have noted, a kind of liberalism that may be termed "religious naturalism," or "theistic naturalism," of which Henry Nelson Wieman is the most distinguished and influential proponent. It aims to be a bridge between the science-centered, John Dewey type of humanistic liberalism and Christian faith. It therefore stresses the empirical method and through it the discovery of God as Creative Good. God is the creative process of growth in meaning and value, immanent in the world and transcendent to man but not to the universe as a whole. In his earlier presentations Professor Wieman made little reference to the Bible, and this view was set forth essentially on philosophical rather than theological grounds. In later years there seems to be more tendency to include biblical concepts such as sin, salvation, and the Kingdom of God within the categories of this position. Nevertheless, it remains primarily a type of philosophy, with the Bible left to one side or subsumed within patterns drawn from another source. The basic point of difference, which makes amalgamation impossible, is its conception of God as a creative, but still as an impersonal, process. And this is *not* what the Bible says!

Twenty years ago this view was making quite a stir, particularly in university circles, and church leaders were interested in it at least to the point of refutation. Now one does not hear much about it. In the attempt to form a bridge between two disparate views, Professor Wieman and his followers have apparently not proved convincing to either group.

[5] It is far more prevalent in university and other intellectual circles than among the rank and file of church people. This is often overlooked in criticisms of liberalism.

I have written elsewhere my estimate of this type of thought,[6] and shall not linger to discuss it further here. We turn now to the liberalism of the churches.

Liberalism is primarily a spirit and a method rather than a body of Christian beliefs. It stands for the spirit of free inquiry and the discovery of God through any channels by which God has made Himself manifest—the Bible, certainly, but the Bible as understood through Christian experience, the history of the Church, and the fullest use we can make of our mental as well as our spiritual faculties. It finds God also in physical nature and in the best insights and strivings of the human persons He has created in His image, and makes no sharp separation among our many God-given pathways to the reality of God.

Within the Bible, liberalism has put its major accent on the life and recorded teachings of Jesus. Accordingly, it has taken seriously the commandment of love, and has tried to extend the range of its application to all society as well as to individuals. For this reason, liberalism has been the chief proponent of the social gospel, now more commonly called in terms less offensive to neo-orthodox ears, "the responsible society."

Liberalism has never broken with evangelism in the sense of witness to the gospel, but it has often been suspicious of revivalism as too emotional, transient in effect, and uncalculated to develop Christian character in the whole of life. It has been a strong proponent of Christian nurture, and most of the religious education scientifically developed within the past half-century has stood on a liberal foundation.

Among all these endeavors and achievements the one which stands out above others is its advocacy of the historical method of studying the Bible. This has been perhaps its most lasting contribution, for no neo-orthodox leader repudiates it; it is the procedure which has most stirred fundamentalism

[6] In *The Recovery of Ideals*, pp. 145-50.

to uneasiness and attack. And it is obviously this aspect of liberalism which is most directly related to the theme of this chapter. We must therefore give it considerable attention.

The historical approach to the Bible is a broader term than textual criticism. The latter, which is the attempt to get the most accurate form of the original writing and the most accurate translation, is a job for specialists only. Its results, however, are interwoven with the attempt to understand the Bible in its original setting, often called its *Sitz im Leben*. The historical method, though it has very extensive ramifications, may be briefly defined as the attempt to discover what has been written in the Bible, by whom and to whom, in what literary forms, when and in what sequence, for what purpose and under what circumstances.

These studies, pursued initially by biblical scholars but taught in the seminaries and gradually being made accessible to laymen, where sympathetically received are of incalculable value both to Christian faith and to biblical theology. They have made the Bible "come alive" to many who saw in it only an antiquated and mysterious book, and they have given added devotional as well as intellectual enrichment to those who already prized the Bible as a guide to Christian living. This approach, without capitulating to rationalism, has made possible the dynamic synthesis of faith and reason which we have said is essential to Christian knowledge.

Why is this so? First, because Christianity is through and through a historical religion. The revelation of God came to the Hebrew people within the events of their social and political existence, and to the people of Palestine in the first century through the birth, ministry, teaching, death, and resurrection of "the Word made flesh" in a particular historical setting. In such a setting the Church was founded, began its witness, collected and canonized the writings which constitute our Bible. It was apparently God's purpose to speak through persons whose lives were set in the midst of events. For Christianity, "word" and "event" are so inter-twined that each requires knowledge of the other for fullest understanding.

Second, we have in the Bible a paradoxical combination. A "strange world," culturally so far removed from our pres-ent age that much of it is not self-explanatory, reflects never-theless perennial human tendencies. We can read the Bible for what it reflects of social and political history from about the fifteenth century B.C. to the second A.D., and find there the growth of Semitic culture from nomadic to agricultural pursuits, from tribal to monarchal to colonial status, from primitive communal independence to great national power and then its loss, from primitive religion through henotheism to monotheism to a faith centered in the God of Jesus Christ. All we can learn about the geographical, economic, political, and cultural setting of the Bible throws light upon what God was saying to the people of the Bible through the events of their history; then through these events and what was writ-ten in response to them, what He is saying *to us*.

And in the third place, a historical understanding of the Bible is not merely a convenient adjunct to biblical theology; it is *essential* to it. Essential, that is, to any right apprehension of it whereby revelation sheds its artificial accretions and its inherited or self-imposed dogmatic forms to become vital, truth-giving, and life-transforming.

This is not to say that the Christian who studies the Bible historically is guaranteed infallible truth, or that no truth can be obtained without it! We have already seen that the conservative and fundamentalist approaches have come out with some true and vital insights which are the common heritage of our Christian faith. Nevertheless, it was a matter of tremendous importance to a Christian doctrine of revela-tion when the historical method of biblical study was in-troduced. Emil Brunner puts it this way:

For the first time in the history of theology, revelation, in its whole historical reality, became the object of theological reflection. This severance from the inherited orthodox-confessional theory, or from the orthodox-traditional view of Scripture, only took place gradually, after much hesitation and misgiving. Thus there arose a new school of thought, characterized by historical realism, which no longer identified revelation with infallible verbal expressions, but went back behind the words of the Bible, to the *facts* themselves.[7]

The past tense, used by Dr. Brunner, is accurate with regard to nearly all the theologians and biblical scholars of our day. Anyone in close touch with the churches knows that there the transition is by no means past, and that the "hesitation and misgiving" are still widely prevalent.

With so great gain from the historical method and its wide sponsorship by liberal Christian leaders, why was this not enough? Part of the answer has been suggested. Not all who espoused this method were sufficiently concerned about biblical theology. Noting the many forms of thought emerging from varied situations within the Bible, some felt doubt as to the existence of a single, or even a dominant, biblical point of view. Diversity there certainly is in the Bible, literary, social, cultural, and religious, and a legitimate protest against an artificial uniformity sometimes blurred the realization of a great unity that centers in God's redemptive love. Discovery of the human factors in the Bible's making, though indispensable to right knowledge of it, sometimes outweighed the Word that God is eternally speaking through it. In short, some who used this method lost sight of the reality and meaning of revelation.

There is no point in affixing blame. Most of those who followed this course did so conscientiously, partly in deference to scientific method in pursuit of truth, partly in counterdefense against a fundamentalist background or current

---

[7] *Revelation and Reason*, pp. 11-12.

fundamentalist attacks. I repeat that I do not believe the leaders of American liberalism ever, to any marked degree, surrendered an interest in biblical theology or threw out revelation under the impact of "higher criticism." Some others did. Some were too cautious to do the educative spade-work necessary to win their people to the historical approach, and so preached a moralistic message. For these and other reasons previously noted, liberalism declined in evangelical vigor.

At this juncture the new orthodoxy swung into power. What, then, does it do with the authority of the Bible?

d. *Neo-orthodoxy.* "Neo-orthodoxy" is too complex a term to be adequately characterized in the amount of space we ought proportionately to give to it. Its primary focus is a re-action against "the modern temper" in Christian thought and a return to (but not a repetition of) certain great notes in the earlier Christian tradition. Neo-Thomism and the work of Berdyaev, Bulgakov, and Florovsky in Russian Orthodoxy are forms of neo-orthodoxy, but we must limit discussion to the Protestant types.

Protestant neo-orthodoxy may be distinguished from the other types of biblical theology we have canvassed both by what it accents and by what it attacks. Affirmatively, it stresses the uniqueness of the Bible as the Word of God (*Heilsgeschichte*), the centrality within it of the revelation of God in Christ, the redemptive aspect of this revelation as its primary fact, the transcendent holiness of God, the sinfulness and inadequacy of man, his perennial need of divine forgiveness and grace, the primacy of faith both for redemption and for the apprehension of revelation. So far, it goes along with the main stream of the Christian tradition, and neither conservative nor liberal ought to quarrel with it.

In its negations, however, it arouses opposition from both ends. Usually proclaimed polemically, it attacks both fundamentalism and liberalism, and thus calls forth counterattacks.

To the malaise of the fundamentalist (once he gets past his initial joy at seeing liberalism castigated!) the neo-orthodox exponent renounces biblical literalism and all its works. Even Karl Barth (who often seems to the liberal to be over-working certain passages to prove his point) lays down as axiomatic the dictum, "These documents, the canonical writings of the Old and New Testaments, are human documents. Since this is so, we are given the unavoidable task of understanding them in a human way, and also enabled to do so." [8] A verbal-inspiration theory of the Bible seems to him not to be good Reformation doctrine, and bound to lead to distortion of the Bible as the Word of God.

Liberalism, however, is the more common object of attack, as being theologically and culturally the more influential perversion of the truth. The elements most inveighed against are liberalism's rationalism, its conformity to the prevailing culture, its optimism about man and the possibilities of human progress, its man-centered activism and moralism, its stress on "the Jesus of history," its utopian (or near-utopian) expectancy of the coming of the Kingdom of God on earth in disregard of biblical eschatology.

Neo-orthodox leaders differ among themselves. Barth, we have noted, will have no truck with natural theology, and writes in his *Dogmatik* hundreds of pages on the doctrine of creation without a look at the world outside the Bible, or at what science tells us of it. Brunner, though suspicious of natural theology when divorced from the saving revelation of God in Christ, finds in the Bible a Christian theology of nature (Rom. 1:19, 32) which he thinks ought to be brought into contact with the orders of existence as we find them. Barth insists that there is one revelation only: namely, the revelation in Jesus Christ (though he goes much farther than do most liberals in questioning the accuracy of the records of the historical Jesus). Brunner finds much more variety in

[8] *The Knowledge of God and the Service of God*, p. 66.

the forms of revelation. Christ, to be sure, is the center, but there is a primitive revelation in the original creation, a prophetic anticipatory revelation, the witness of the apostles in the New Testament, the subsequent preaching and teaching of the Church, the witness of the Holy Spirit, a final eschatological revelation to come at the end of history.

The last point calls for an attempt to say briefly what neo-orthodoxy does with the concept of myth. Liberalism has long contended that there are myths in the Bible, such as those of the Garden of Eden and the Tower of Babel, which are not literal history but are more than fanciful legends; i.e., they are primitive attempts in story form to state eternal truth. Though not consciously designed, like Plato's myths, to state such truth pictorially, they may still do so, and be a vehicle of divine revelation. They ought, therefore, neither to be discredited as primitive folklore nor taken as history, but read for the permanent truth God is speaking through them. "In the beginning God created the heavens and the earth" is true, regardless of the fact that the first chapter of Genesis is not a scientifically accurate account of the mode of His creation.

Neo-orthodoxy accepts this principle but extends it to certain central New Testament concepts to speak of the myth (or *mythos*) of the Resurrection and of Christ's final coming in glory, which liberals usually either accept or reject as historical fact. The biblical accounts of these events, proclaiming the suprarational fact of the redemption of sinful humanity through Christ, it is said, ought not to be compressed into rational categories. To attempt it is to distort their great meaning, apprehensible only to faith. Neo-orthodoxy thus objects both to the literalizing of the biblical language and to the "demythologizing" advocated by Rudolf Bultmann to translate its meaning into terms congenial to the modern mind. This had much to do with the pre-Evanston controversy over the eschatological meaning of "Christ—the hope of the world."

Both Brunner and Niebuhr are more concerned than Barth to communicate the gospel to modern man and apply it to the manifold problems of Christian decision. Both have written extensively on Christian ethics and have a wide hearing outside the churches. While all three draw their message primarily from the letters of Paul rather than the Synoptic Gospels, Niebuhr has the broader sweep both as to sources of Christian thought and its applications.

Space permits only a brief word of evaluation. What was noted several paragraphs back as the affirmations of neo-orthodoxy are great affirmations, so central to the Christian faith that liberalism owes it a major debt for recalling Christian leadership to a sense of their importance. Reasons have already been given for justifying the neo-orthodox repudiation of verbal inspiration and biblical literalism.

It is, however, at the point of negations and aspersions upon liberal theology that questions must be raised. For one thing, it is often a "straw man" liberal—or at best a John Dewey type of liberal—that is set up to be knocked down. Liberals in the churches have not, for the most part, forgotten about sin, relied wholly on reason or scientific method, or been utopian in their expectations as to what they themselves or mankind as a whole apart from God could accomplish.[9] For another thing, neo-orthodoxy in its legitimate stress on the Bible as the fountainhead of Christian theology has often centered too exclusively on those parts of the Bible congenial to its own position and has drawn less upon the Bible as a whole than has the liberal mind.

A third defect, not in the field of Christian knowledge but of Christian experience, is the disparity between a constant stress on redemption and a very slight recognition that the

[9] Note, for example, what Walter Rauschenbusch says of the kingdom of evil in *A Theology for the Social Gospel*, chap. ix.

redeemed life is empirically different from the unredeemed. So eager are the exponents of this school to stress human sinfulness, even in the best of Christians, and our constant need of divine grace, that grace does not appear actually to have made much difference! [10] Paul had a greater sense of moral victory through Christ than is found in most of the writings of this school.

3. Is synthesis possible?

We must draw this chapter to a close by seeing what can be put together from all these conscientiously held but disparate forms of biblical theology. Is any synthesis possible?

Among the conservative, liberal, and neo-orthodox approaches there is enough in common so that in local churches, denominations, and the ecumenical movement Christians are working together in fellowship. The fundamentalist mind is by nature dissident—that is why we have seen fit to distinguish it from the conservative—and because of its dissidence there can be little meeting ground. The most that can be hoped for at present is some increased understanding of what the fundamentalist is trying to defend which makes him take the course he does.

Fortunately an admirable statement has already been formulated which states the essential grounds on which leading American, European, and Asian scholars have reached agreement. These "Guiding Principles for the Interpretation of the Bible" were agreed upon by an ecumenical Study Conference held in Oxford in the summer of 1949, printed by the Study Department of the World Council in a pamphlet entitled *The Bible and the Church's Message,* and later enlarged in a full-length volume, *Biblical Authority for Today,* edited by Wolfgang Schweitzer and Alan Richardson.

In general, the position is that of the *Heilsgeschichte,*

---

[10] See Daniel Day Williams' *God's Grace and Man's Hope* for an admirable analysis of this defect.

which is basic to the neo-orthodox position but increasingly accepted by liberals—the uniqueness of the Bible as revelatory, of God's redemptive activity in history, the Word of God to him who will listen to that Word in faith. But faith is not credulity; nor its mood bigotry. The "necessary theological presuppositions of biblical interpretation" are thus summarized:

A. It is agreed that the Bible is our common starting point, for there God's Word confronts us, a Word which humbles the hearers so that they are more ready to listen and to discuss than they are to assert their own opinions.

B. It is agreed that the primary message of the Bible concerns God's gracious and redemptive activity for the saving of sinful man that He might create in Jesus Christ a new people for Himself. . . .

C. It is agreed that the starting point of the Christian interpreter lies within the redeemed community of which by faith he is a member.

D. It is agreed that the center and goal of the whole Bible is Jesus Christ. This gives the two Testaments a perspective in which Jesus Christ is seen both as the fulfillment and the end of the law.

E. It is agreed that the unity of the Old and the New Testament is not to be found in any naturalistic development, or in any static identity, but in the ongoing redemptive activity of God in the history of one people, reaching its fulfillment in Christ. . . .

F. It is agreed that allegorical interpretations which are not intended by the biblical authors are arbitrary and their use may be a disservice to the proper recognition of biblical authority. . . .

G. It is agreed that although we may differ in the manner in which tradition, reason and natural law may be used in the interpretation of Scripture, any teaching that clearly contradicts the biblical position cannot be accepted as Christian.[11]

[11] *The Bible and the Church's Message,* pp. 11-12.

Thus far a fundamentalist might agree, and a liberal ought to! The next section of the statement, however, comes out squarely for the historical method of study. In an analysis of the interpretation of a specific passage the assembled scholars agreed to this:

A. It is agreed that one must start with an historical and critical examination of the passage. This includes:
1. The determination of the text;
2. The literary form of the passage;
3. The historical situation, the *Sitz im Leben;*
4. The meaning which the words had for the original author and hearer or reader;
5. The understanding of the passage in the light of its total context and the background out of which it emerged.

B. It is agreed that in the case of an Old Testament passage, one must examine and expound it in relation to the revelation of God to Israel both before and after its own period. Then the interpreter should turn to the New Testament in order to view the passage in that perspective. . . .

C. It is agreed that in the case of a New Testament passage one should examine it in the light of its setting and context; then turn to the Old Testament to discover its background in God's former revelation. Returning again to the New Testament one is able to see and expound the passage in the light of the whole scope of *Heilsgeschichte.*[12]

We need carry this citation no further. It is clear that in spite of admitted differences, there is a great agreement among outstanding Christian scholars of today. To summarize these agreements, the Bible is the Word of God, a *Heilsgeschichte* bearing central witness to the Christian community of God's redemptive activity, and this witness can only be read aright when the best procedures of historical and textual criticism are linked with faith.

And this, after all, is the dynamic synthesis of faith and reason for which I have been asking throughout this book!

[12] *Ibid.,* pp. 12-13.

CHAPTER VI

The Inner Light of the Spirit

WE SHALL ATTEMPT IN THIS CHAPTER TO DISCUSS THREE AP-
proaches to Christian knowledge which have a common
center and in some aspects are identical, in others disparate.
These are the inner witness of the Holy Spirit, the spiritual
life in its many-sided totality, and the mystic's way. Not only
do these merge into one another without being synonymous,
but each one of the three is a somewhat indeterminate concept, variously understood by various Christians. Lack of
precision characterizes most discussions of any one of these
concepts, and to attempt to say something about all three of
them is to flirt with trouble!

Nevertheless, I shall attempt it. All three are immensely
important, and at least the first two are regarded by most
Christians as indispensable. Mysticism would be in better
standing if it were better understood. We shall not try to say
all that anybody ever has thought, or could think, about any
of them, but what the author thinks. This may narrow the
scope of inquiry to manageable compass.

1. *The Holy Spirit*

The Holy Spirit may be understood either theologically
or experientially. We are here mainly concerned with the
second of these contexts, and with the experience of a sense
of "witness" from the Holy Spirit which seems to the Christian to give him authentic knowledge, light, or guidance.
The two approaches are intertwined, for without a sense of
Divine Presence the doctrine of the third person of the
Trinity would not have emerged in the thought of the early

church, and if the doctrine had not been carried through the centuries as a basic element in Christian faith, the problems of knowledge at this point would very likely have taken a different turn.

Biblical scholars are generally agreed that there is no explicit doctrine of the Trinity in the Bible, though there are foregleams of it in the apostolic benediction of II Cor. 13:14 and in the baptismal formula of the Great Commission found at the end of the Gospel of Matthew. There are, however, numerous references to the Spirit, or to the Spirit of God. In the Old Testament, and in many of the New Testament passages,[1] these terms are used as if to say "God expressing Himself in action" or "God present within the world." In the great and familiar prayer of Ps. 51:11:

> Cast me not away from thy presence,
> and take not thy holy Spirit from me,

it is significant that "holy" is simply a descriptive adjective, written with a small "h."

However, in the New Testament we begin to find the Holy Spirit referred to as an entity, and as meaning not only the Spirit of God but the presence of the Risen Christ. It is significant that in the earliest New Testament writings, Paul's Letters, Paul seems to use interchangeably the terms "Holy Spirit," "the Spirit of God," "the Spirit of Christ," or simply "Christ" or "the Lord" or "the Spirit." [2] This implicit identification becomes explicit in the assertion in II Cor. 3:17, "Now the Lord is the Spirit."

Is the Holy Spirit "he" or "it"? Current usage justifies both pronouns, and if we look sharply at the New Testament, we shall find there justification for both. Where Paul is stressing

[1] For example, Gen. 1:2; Neh. 9:20; Ps. 104:30; 139:7; Matt. 4:1; 12:28; Luke 4:18.

[2] See, for example, Rom. 5:5; 8:2, 4-16, 26, 27; 14:17; I Cor. 2:10-16; Eph. 3:14-19; Phil. 1:19; I Thess. 1:5, 6.

the saving, enlightening activity of God in Christ, the reference is personal, though usually without clear distinction as to whether the Spirit is "the Lord" or what the Lord does. The Holy Spirit as a person comes to clearest expression in the Gospel of John, where it is stated that Jesus promised that upon His going away would come the Counselor, "even the Spirit of truth," the Holy Spirit, to be sent by the Father in His name to teach His followers all things and to be with them forever (14:16, 17, 25, 26). However, there are numerous passages both in the Gospels and in Acts where the Holy Spirit appears to be the *gift* of God to Jesus or to His followers, as in the coming of the Holy Spirit upon Jesus at his baptism or to the waiting disciples on the day of Pentecost. Not only Jesus but others are said to have been "filled with the Holy Spirit." [3] In this setting it seems to have been identical with the grace or the power of God.

What this indicates is that within the period covered by the New Testament there was no clear differentiation of the Holy Spirit into the third person of the Trinity; yet in a vital way the Spirit was felt to bring to Christians the presence and power of God in Christ. From the standpoint of Christian experience this is still its meaning.

It was when the Trinity began to be defined as *una substantia tres personae,* and the *personae* came to be thought of, not as three manifestations of one God, but as three persons in the ordinary sense, that tritheism crept into the thinking of the Church. Since this problem belongs mainly in the field of Christology, we shall not discuss it here except to say that the Trinity is a valid, even an essential, Christian doctrine, while tritheism is not. The Holy Spirit is not some third deity. Yet the Holy Spirit, as the Spirit of God incarnate within Jesus Christ and present with us as the Living Christ, is a reality. It is this that we are concerned with in this study.

In our discussion of the Holy Spirit as the Divine Presence,

[3] See, for example, Luke 1:15, 41, 67; 4:1; Acts 2:4; 4:31; 6:3, 5; 9:17.

an inner witness to the truth God is seeking to reveal, we shall attempt like the first Christians to think of this Presence as experience rather than doctrine. If the view of revelation set forth in chapter 4 is accepted, we shall not at any point expect the Holy Spirit to give us theology full-blown. If our findings regarding the authority of the Bible are sound, the *testimonium Spiritus Sancti* may give us light in interpretation, as the Reformers maintained, but it will not be the kind of light that can replace honest, patient historical inquiry. What the Holy Spirit, rightly accepted in Christian experience, will do for us is to vivify our Christian living, sensitize our hearts, open our minds to the best possible use of all the faculties God has given us. As one of the widely used modern creeds puts it with simplicity and power: "We believe in the Holy Spirit as the Divine Presence in our lives, whereby we are kept in perpetual remembrance of the truth of Christ, and find strength and help in time of need." [4]

The term "witness of the Spirit" as a distinctive emphasis within the Methodism of John Wesley and his followers means neither a set of dogmas to be accepted nor an atomistic view of the multitudinous decisions of daily life. Its main stress is on the inner assurance of personal salvation, an assurance which Wesley lacked before his Aldersgate experience and which thereafter gave him immeasurable power. Out of this all-encompassing witness came confidence and strength to act with a sense of divine leading, but never with any surrender of the obligation to use to the full whatever powers of decision, speech, or action he possessed.

Such an assurance of guidance by the Spirit is a vital part of Christian experience, even when it is not explicitly stressed, in any household of faith. But it is not without its problems.

The most crucial problem, whether with reference to the inclusive act of "being saved" or the many acts and decisions

[4] *The Methodist Hymnal,* p. 512.

that come in the course of the Christian life, is to distinguish the voice of the Holy Spirit from one's own subconscious impulses, egoistic desires, and faulty rationalizations. A cataclysmic emotional experience by no means authenticates conversion, even when one feels radically changed. And on the assumption of being led by the Spirit, Christians have more than once slandered or slain each other, and have done "all manner of evil" which a more sober Christian judgment could hardly think contributory to the Kingdom. There is a kind of moral dullness which the Spirit seems often not to challenge.[5] The borderline between fanaticism on the one hand, and a prophetic or evangelical urgency on the other, is a tenuous one. When the guidance of the Spirit is claimed for all such courses, how distinguish what is truly the voice of God?

The story of the giving of the Holy Spirit on the day of Pentecost, as recorded in the second chapter of Acts, has much to teach us at this point. Let us look at it in some detail.

When the Spirit came to Peter and the Twelve, and through them to three thousand souls on the day of Pentecost, it came (1) on a foundation, (2) to the receptive, (3) with life-transforming power, (4) in and to the Christian fellowship, (5) with an exacting requirement, and (6) with significant fruit in life and action. The Holy Spirit still so comes.

The foundation on which the Holy Spirit came to the first Christians on that momentous day was an objective, dependable, and authentic prior revelation. Part of this foundation was their inherited Jewish faith, familiar through the Scriptures and woven into their being. But the all-important part of it was the life, works, death, and resurrection of Jesus. Peter in his great address could appropriately appeal

---

[5] With all due regard for Wesley's great Christian dedication, a recent rereading of his *Journal* convinces me that he was far from being "perfect in love" with reference to his wife!

to the prophecy of Joel as a background; the foreground was "Jesus of Nazareth, a man attested to you by God with mighty works and wonders and signs which God did through him in your midst, as you yourselves know" (Acts 2:22). It was, as Paul put it elsewhere, "the light of the knowledge of the glory of God in the face of Christ" (II Cor. 4:6), that shone in their hearts that day to make them receptive to the Spirit and clear in their discernment of it.

And, to the present, this is the truest test of when the Spirit speaks. "Let this mind be in you, which was also in Christ Jesus" (Phil. 2:5, K.J.V.) [6] is at the same time the objective foundation for the Christian's reception of the Spirit and the objective criterion by which to test the inner voice. Does this accord with what Jesus was, taught, did? This is the first question to ask about any supposed leading of the Spirit. If the answer is no, we need go no further.

A second characteristic, we noted, was that the Spirit came to the receptive. It was on the day of the Jewish festival that celebrated the close of the harvest season, fifty days after the Passover, that they were "all together in one place." The story does not explicitly say that they were there expecting and waiting for the Spirit;[7] in fact, it was "suddenly" that the great experience swept over their souls. Nevertheless, the paradox of grace is exactly this—that only he who seeks finds it, and when it is found, it seems to come with amazing power from beyond one's self.

Nobody, today or in any day, can be led of the Spirit against his will, though he may long feel its impulses stirring him, as Paul felt himself in his persecuting days "kick against the goads" and Francis Thompson in immortal verse recounts pursuit by "the Hound of Heaven." It is equally true that nobody, by his own compulsive effort, can conjure up

---

[6] The King James rendering here is more forceful than R.S.V.
[7] But cf. Acts 1:4-8.

the Holy Spirit. God speaks, but he who would hear must wait and listen.

And in the third place, when the Spirit fell upon those early Christians, all of life was different. It came with tremendous emotional power that made them feel they could not be silent! Today, "speaking with tongues" is not its usual or its best accompaniment. But witness is, and this witness is bound to seem to an astonished world, if not like intoxication, at least like queerness. Whether the reaction comes in persecuting mobs such as John Wesley had to contend with, or in being cited as "subversive," or simply in an incredulous smile with a lifting of eyebrows, the emotional effects of the Spirit-filled life are bound to be both rewarding and costing. But when is the cost rightly borne in spite of opposition? The answer is suggested at the end of the story of Pentecost—in willingness to share not only one's prayers and praises but also one's possessions for the love of God in Christ.

Fourth, the Spirit came in and to the *koinonia*. Christianity is through and through a social religion. This is not to say that the Spirit never speaks in solitude. We are advised on the best authority: "When you pray, go into your room and shut the door and pray to your Father who is in secret; and your Father who sees in secret will reward you" (Matt. 6:6).

But these words of Jesus are a protest against display in religion, not against its corporate foundations. It is the same Jesus who "went to the synagogue, as his custom was, on the sabbath day," that is the Lord of the Church. The Spirit was given in a fellowship; it has always been carried forward in a fellowship. Solitary Christianity, save for those exceptional cases where one must stand alone in defense of a corporate faith, is a contradiction in terms.

This has two important deductions for our guidance in our time. The first is that the Church, through its Christian nurture and proclamation of the gospel, is the natural medium for the coming of the Spirit. It seldom, if ever, comes otherwise. The upbuilding of the Body of Christ of which Paul speaks is also the opening of the main artery through which the life stream of the Spirit can come to its individual members.

The second deduction is the importance of corporate guidance in crucial decisions. This is why the Church must have conferences and councils. It is also the reason why a perplexed Christian, though he alone must make the final decision, does well to seek the counsel of wiser and more experienced fellow Christians. Such counseling ought never to be authoritarian; it can be immensely helpful as a medium by which through the removal of dust clouds and the discovery of wider implications, the Holy Spirit's leading can be discerned with greater clarity.

Fifth, there is a stringent—and to many souls a too costly—requirement. Peter minced no words about it. When the listeners to his sermon, "cut to the heart," cried out, "Brethren, what shall we do?" his answer was unequivocal. "And Peter said to them, 'Repent, and be baptized every one of you in the name of Jesus Christ for the forgiveness of your sins; and you shall receive the gift of the Holy Spirit.' " (Acts 2:38.)

Repentance is as much a requirement today as it ever was. And our age, which minimizes the reality of sin and wants to get what it can as easily as possible, does not make much of repentance. Of torturing remorse, which is a combination of self-pity, fear of consequences, and smitings of conscience, there is much—and every psychiatrist must deal with it. But to repentance in the Christian sense of humble acknowledgment of sin before God and earnest effort by His help to put it from us, our secular world is singularly obtuse.

Such sensitizing of the soul through repentance is one of the prime requirements of that spiritual discernment which makes possible the coming of the Holy Spirit to the inner life. Traditional Christian thought has set us a sequence within which God creates, Christ redeems, the Holy Spirit sanctifies. It is not necessary to limit our thought to such a sequence, but the agency of the Spirit in the growth of the Christian soul through continued repentance and repeated expressions of divine forgiveness is a true insight. Any doctrine of sanctification which assumes the attainment on earth of a state of static perfection gets off base, and needs to hear again the word of Paul, "Let any one who thinks that he stands take heed lest he fall" (I Cor. 10:12).

Baptism in the name of Jesus as a formal, ecclesiastical act is not the basic requirement. Quakers are Christians without it, and no group has been more sensitive to the Spirit! Baptism of soul through repentance for sin and immersion in the infinite grace of God *is* a requirement. So exacting is it that many prefer not to meet it, then wonder why they cannot feel God's presence.

And, in the sixth place, the coming of the Holy Spirit is related to the whole of life. Not only does it call for the surrender of all we are; it bears fruit in all we are. The story in Acts would have been incomplete had not the Spirit changed the mode of life of those early Christians. To have all things in common, to sell their possessions and goods and distribute them to all, as any had need—this can easily be branded as impractical, but hardly as unchristian! There is a great lift, which many today in greater opulence might envy, in the words:

And day by day, attending the temple together and breaking bread in their homes, they partook of food with glad and generous hearts, praising God and having favor with all the people. And the Lord added to their number day by day those who were being saved (Acts 2:46-47).

Yet the sequel to the coming of the Spirit does not lie in this second chapter of Acts. It is throughout the book of

Acts, and throughout Paul's Letters, and all through the history of the Church. It is found in the "faith, hope, and love" of Christians everywhere. Paul has stated for us in matchless words this fruit of the Spirit:

> But the fruit of the Spirit is love, joy, peace, patience, kindness, goodness, faithfulness, gentleness, self-control; against such there is no law. And those who belong to Christ Jesus have crucified the flesh with its passions and desires.
> If we live by the Spirit, let us also walk by the Spirit (Gal. 5:22-25).

The fruit of the Spirit, furthermore, is the final test of reality in the distinguishing of its true appearance from illusion. One who does not "walk by the Spirit" may claim ever so volubly to be Spirit-filled, even sanctified, but the claim will inevitably be under suspicion. One may bear fruit without saying much about it, as is usually the way of humble Christians who are "the salt of the earth," and be living witnesses to the divine Presence.

Such fruit-bearing is the keynote of "the spiritual life." To this often ambiguous term we must now give further attention.

2. *The spiritual life*

The spiritual life is talked about a great deal today, and there seems to be a resurgence of interest in it. Its earlier designation, the life of Christian "piety," has gone out of fashion, and many recoil from the term as if it meant either sanctimoniousness or a state of innocuous nonentity in things spiritual. Whatever it is called, it is a permanent but not an easily definable aspect of the Christian religion.

Few would question the importance of the spiritual life as a constructive, supporting, and vital part of Christian experience. Our main concern at this point is not with its cultivation or its fruits; I have dealt with this in *Prayer and the Common Life.* Its relevance to the problem of this book lies in the question of how much true knowledge, if any, it yields. Opinions range all the way from the assumption that the life of prayer gives so much assurance that it makes theology unnecessary to a rejection of pietism as too subjectivistic to be in any sense trustworthy.

What is the spiritual life? The term has three recognizable meanings which merge into one another without being identical. The broadest of these is "the life of the spirit"—the spirit being conceived as that aspect of personality which is nonphysical and nonmaterial. The spirit in this sense includes man's intellectual capacities and all that makes him a rational being, but with the particular stress falling not on his cognitive pursuits but his value judgments—his loves and loyalties, hopes, desires, and moral decisions. In this sense "the spiritual" is by no means an exclusively religious category. Humanists and secular idealists, along with the convinced exponents of Christian faith, prize the life of the spirit and seek to enrich and enhance it.

The narrowest of the three meanings limits it to prayer, worship, the reading of the Bible or other devotional materials, and such conscious efforts as these to strengthen the inner life through communion with God. The modes vary widely, as do the effects in the worshiper, but all center in the attempt to be nourished in the life of prayer.

The third meaning equates the spiritual life with religious experience. For the Christian it then means his entire life as a Christian—his acting as well as his praying, his conduct in his job and his family as well as in church and in his moments of private prayer—but all viewed from the standpoint of his relation to God in Christ. This is what the spiritual life ought to mean if it is not to be too departmentalized. It is, however, not so common in current Christian usage as the second meaning just outlined. The sacredness of the common life, which was an essential principle of Reforma-

tion Protestantism, is only now after long lapse beginning
to be recovered.

A word must now be said about the relation of each of
these to Christian knowledge.

The life of the spirit, in the first sense, is essential to the
pursuit of any knowledge, Christian or otherwise. In the
general presuppositions of knowledge outlined at the end of
chapter 2, we found that the discovery of knowledge is a
function of our total experience, not of intellectual processes
alone. We found also that values are facts, as "existential" a
part of human existence as anything that can be more precisely analyzed and charted through scientific method. All
that has been said in the earlier chapters of this book bears on
the approach to truth through the life of the spirit as the
apprehension of reality through a dynamic union of faith
with reason. I shall not attempt, therefore, to recanvass this
ground.

The second meaning of the spiritual life can be more
precisely designated by the term "the devotional life." As
we shall note presently, it has close affinities with mysticism
when mysticism is itself broadly enough defined, but many
who would recoil in horror at the idea of being mystics
still grant the validity and necessity of Christian prayer.
Through it come guidance, strength, motivating power for
Christian living, and even those Christians who do not
themselves often pray are usually ready to acknowledge that
they would be better Christians if they did.

It gives guidance, we just said. But "guidance" too is suspect! It calls to mind courses of triviality, abnormality, or
fanaticism to which Christians have sometimes thought themselves guided, while other, more hardheaded Christians have
had their grave doubts. When is guidance real?

There is no inflexible rule by which to distinguish with
automatic precision between God's answer to prayer as we
seek for light, and our own subconscious impulses. Never-

theless, all that was said in the preceding section about the voice of the Holy Spirit is here applicable. The first requirement is willingness to be led by the Spirit of God as this Spirit has come to us in Jesus Christ. The first criterion, therefore, is whether any impulse that seems to come in response to prayer accords with what Jesus was and did and taught. In a word, "Is it Christian?" Beyond this, among various courses that might seem to be Christian, the choice must be made with openness of sensitivity, the best use possible of our God-given powers of reason, and willingness to obey. "If any man's will is to do his [God's] will, he shall know whether the teaching is from God" (John 7:17) is a principle of eternal validity but not one to be taken out of context. Jesus is recorded as having spoken these words to validate his authority from God; our knowledge of what God is seeking to teach us requires both the objective authority of Jesus and our own willing obedience to what God sets before us.

We have been speaking mainly of matters of personal moral decision in which light is sought from God through prayer. But what of "the teaching" in a more theological sense? Of certainty of the reality of God? And of light as to His nature? Here we must walk carefully, for it is easy to make a mistake in either direction.

First, it must be said that the devotional life is no substitute for theology. To try to substitute praying for hard thinking is fatal to both pursuits. Our Lord has enjoined to "love the Lord your God with all your . . . *mind.*" We shall not "know of the teaching" unless we attend to it not only in obedience of will and fervency of spirit, but with the best use we can make of all the mental capacities God has given us.

Second, the devotional life *does* open the mind to fresh insights, enlarge horizons, uncover hidden aspects of truth. We have stressed the fact that for a true approach to theology,

129

one must stand within the faith he seeks to systematize. It is possible to go further and say that for a right apprehension of this faith, the devotional life must be sensitive and strong.[8] Sterility at this point is bound to cloud the mind and the spirit to essential insights into the nature and reality of God. "The unspiritual man," says Paul, "does not receive the gifts of the Spirit of God, for they are folly to him, and he is not able to understand them because they are spiritually discerned." (I Cor. 2:14.)

Of the spiritual life in the third sense, that of total religious living, I shall make only two observations, both of which are in the nature of cautions. The first is to beware of divorcing the devotional life from this wider context. When this is done, prayer becomes an emotional luxury or a cloak for egocentricity instead of being a channel of both light and power from God. Against such a divorce, and its tendency to a pharisaic ostentation in prayer, Jesus repeatedly warned.

The second is the need to beware against supposing that the Christian life in general can be vital and light-bearing in neglect of the devotional life. It can be conventionally moral, highly respectable, even to a considerable degree altruistic, without it. But it cannot be the Kingdom-seeking, cross-bearing, richly fruitful life that God requires of the men of Christian faith. And without this quality, the light of faith tends ever to flicker as the winds of life blow upon it.

3. The way of mysticism

Mysticism takes so many forms that it is a term extremely difficult to define. America's greatest exponent of mysticism, Rufus M. Jones, thus defines it in *The Dictionary of Philosophy:*

[8] The implications of this fact are developed at length by Douglas Steere in *On Beginning from Within,* chap. IV.

Mysticism in its simplest and most essential meaning is a type of religion which puts the emphasis on immediate awareness of relation to God, direct and intimate consciousness of Divine Presence. It is religion in its most acute, intense and living stage. . . .

It is not historically sound to find the *essentia* of Mysticism in ecstasy, or in a *via negativa,* or in some kind of esoteric *knowledge,* or in mysterious "communications." The essentia of Mysticism is the experience of direct communion with God.

The limitations suggested in the second paragraph quoted require further explanation. The term has often been loosely and incorrectly used to apply to clairvoyance, crystal gazing, and all sorts of occult "psychic" phenomena. Of such debasing of a good word we shall say nothing here except to repudiate it.

On a somewhat higher plane, but still not in a Christian or distinctly religious context, the term is applied to claims of "knowledge" of an esoteric or theosophical nature. The mystic assumes to have "divine wisdom" which others do not have. Because of this usage the scientific mind not infrequently dismisses as mysticism all metaphysical or religious knowledge not arrived at by scientific method. Though the term in this context may be spoken either with respect or with contempt, this usage carries with it the connotation that the truth-claims of mysticism are not subject to any testing from beyond themselves.

Mysticism in the religious, and particularly in the Christian, sense is neither of these dubious procedures. But within the Christian tradition there are two main types of mysticism, meeting at a common center of the immediate confrontation of the human soul with God, and widely differing at other points. These are the *via negativa,* or negation mysticism, on the one hand, and on the other, what Rufus Jones calls "affirmation mysticism." [9] The two types are also to

[9] Cf. *The Testimony of the Soul,* chap. x.

be distinguished as "union" and "communion" mysticism.

The *via negativa,* stemming from the writings of Dionysius in the fifth century A.D.,[10] stresses the utter transcendence of God, the incapacity of the human mind to know the divine by any ordinary channels, the need to strip off all personal and social entanglements and grounds of dependence and in an ecstatic vision of brief but effulgent glory, become one with the Divine Being. The *scala perfectionis,* or ladder of perfection for this upward climb along the negative way, has three stages: purification, illumination, and union. The first two, involving the purging of the soul so that the pure in heart may see God and the centering of the mind in rapt contemplation upon deity, requires in the worshiper an act of will and often prolonged disciplines. The third, the blessed consummation, is the gift of divine grace.

This type is often referred to as classical mysticism, and William James's analysis of it in *The Varieties of Religious Experience* is frequently quoted. He defines the principal traits of such mystical experience as ineffability, a noetic quality, transiency, and passivity.[11] Though the mystic never can describe in words what has grasped him in the blessed moment of union with the Eternal, he is convinced that from this experience has come knowledge that nothing can disprove, and that needs no further validation.

It is true that this type of mysticism repeatedly appears in the Christian tradition. The anonymous *Cloud of Unknowing* from the fourteenth century is an important literary expression of it, as are the writings of St. John of the Cross and others. Yet it was never the dominant type. Many like Francis of Assisi show some aspects of it in terms of unquestioning trust and ecstatic joy in communion with God, but

[10] Long called "Dionysius the Areopagite" on the assumption that he was the Dionysius of Acts 17:34; now generally referred to as Pseudo-Dionysius.
[11] Pp. 380-81.

still stress *communion* rather than union, and fellowship with men rather than withdrawal.

The second type, which I am convinced is the more normative as well as the more wholesome type, is exemplified at its best by Rufus Jones himself. It is the type which is dominant in the Quaker tradition, and outside the Quaker fellowship is a common possession of many Christians who might not call themselves mystics. It is simply a heightened sense of the need and possibility of communion with God in prayer. It merges by indistinguishable stages with what we have called the devotional life. Its central note, as stated above, is "the emphasis on immediate awareness of relation with God, direct and intimate consciousness of Divine Presence."

This kind of mysticism never assumes that even momentarily God and man become one, save in unity of will and purpose. It finds God within the soul, and in other men, and throughout His world, but the Divine Presence is always—to quote Emile Boutroux's familiar phrase—"the Beyond that is within." Most exponents of this type stress the radiance, joy, and illumination that can come from such fellowship with God, but are wary of ecstasies and claims to esoteric wisdom. Some, like Rufus Jones and Baron von Hügel, have been men of great intellectual stature; others are folk of simple faith unversed in philosophy or theology. In general, however, there is a dual stress both on the need of using all available "pathways to the reality of God" and on the particular illumination and power that come through personal fellowship with God in prayer.

What validity has either of these approaches in terms of Christian knowledge? The answer, for the most part, has been suggested in the two preceding sections. The *via negativa,* by its exclusiveness, is particularly open to the fallacy of seeing what one desires to see or expects to see, and thus of distorting one's own subconscious promptings into visions

133

and voices which seem to the mystic to come unmistakably from God. While some saints of great good works and sensitive Christian insight have followed this path, it has also bred excesses of asceticism, trance, and rapture that are neither morally nor psychologically wholesome. It had better not be cultivated.

The second type, with a sane and normal balance of prayer with thought and of prayer with Christian action, has everything to commend it. It sensitizes, heightens, and mellows the total Christian experience of the mystic, and stirs him both to more devoted service and to more eager search for the truth God stands ready to reveal. The immediacy of his sense of the Divine Presence makes him very sure of God, but does not cancel the obligation to ratify his faith by every available channel.

Certain basic assumptions are made by both types. These are of the need of personal purity, the confidence that God is and may be found, the presence of a Divine Seed, or Spark, or Ground within every man, the possibility of personal, immediate confrontation with the Divine. These are postulates assumed without proof, though no mystic devises them *de novo*. He gets them from his Christian past, in which the Bible has no small part. If they are false assumptions, mysticism collapses. If they are true, mysticism of the communion type is a major source of access to the knowledge of God through personal encounter.

Those who decry mysticism usually do so either in revulsion from the abnormal phenomena sometimes appearing in the *via negativa,* or in the belief that mysticism is antisocial, or on charges of monistic or immanental if not pantheistic trends in its theology. The first charge may be admitted if it is recognized that not all mysticism is of this type. The second is for the most part based on a misunderstanding of mysticism throughout the course of Christian history. Not only the Quakers today, but also a host of saints of the past, have been foremost in their relief of human suffering, impelled thereto by a divine urgency. The third is partly true, more largely false. Mysticism does not lie in the same bed with that type of neo-orthodoxy which stresses the utter transcendence of God and refuses to affirm what George Fox called "that of God in every man." Yet it recognizes the separateness—even the man-made separation—between man and God until by earnest efforts at moral purity, faithful obedience, and costing receptivity the barriers to divine grace are removed and the worshiper discerns with a sense of immediacy the Divine Presence.

Such a divine-human encounter, occurring in the inner recesses of the soul in periods of silent waiting before God, never with bombast or ostentation but with humble trust, every Christian needs to have. And the world needs it immensely. This is true whether this inner immediacy of confrontation be called the witness and leading of the Holy Spirit, or the "practice of the presence of God" in the devotional life, or the mystic's way. If God is found by the inner light of His Spirit, both His reality and His call to the loving service of mankind are unequivocal. If God is not thus found, any other finding is likely to be barren and unfruitful.

CHAPTER VII

The Authority of the Christian Community

W<small>E COME NOW TO A DISCUSSION OF AN APPROACH TO CHRIS-</small>tian truth which is at the same time indispensable and at almost every turn fraught with ambiguity. This is the approach through the pronouncements and the life, experience, and practice of the Christian Church. I have left it to the last because in one sense it is the most basic, yet it carries with it the least agreement, of all the sources of authority.

It is not difficult to see why this is so. The Church is, of course, not more basic than its Lord—whenever it becomes so, it loses its birthright and ceases to be in a true sense a Church. Yet it is through the Church, as the Body of Christ on earth and within the stream of history, that we know our Lord and feel ourselves summoned to be His followers. If the Church does not proclaim a true gospel, the word of Christ to our day is muted or distorted.

Neither is the Church more basic than the Bible, which all Christians have in common, or than the Holy Spirit, through whose presence all need to find power and light. But both individual Christians and those groups of Christians who constitute the churches differ exceedingly as to their interpretation of the Bible and as to what the Holy Spirit says to the churches. Within this variation we cannot simply go our own way regardless of the Church, and neither can we—unless we belong to a highly authoritarian church— put our minds in moth balls or in strait-jackets.

Theology, as we said earlier and must not forget, is the

systematic examination and interpretation of the inherited faith of the Christian community. The faith of our fathers, not only of those whose words and deeds are recorded in the Bible but of sixty generations of Christians since Pentecost, is what theology is made of. Outside the Church we might conceivably devise some helpful philosophy of religion or ethics, but we should have no theology. Yet theology is a process, not a static compendium of past thinking, and no one who wishes either to keep his own mind alert or to serve the present generation can be content with a faith "which was once for all delivered to the saints" (Jude 3).

A word may be in order as to why the chapter is entitled "The Authority of the Christian Community" rather than "The Authority of the Church." What is meant, of course, is not the secular, semi-Christian geographical locality in which we reside, though this has its own authority, partly Christian, partly pagan or nondescript. The Christian community means the *koinonia,* or fellowship of Christians, now nearly world-wide in scope, which in the midst of great variations in national, economic, and social status embraces those "who profess and call themselves Christians." Great variations exist within their forms of worship and of polity as well as theology, but there is a central unity in a common loyalty to Christ and attempt to be Christ's followers. I shall not hesitate to speak of this *koinonia* as the Church, but "the authority of the Church" so quickly suggests either a hierarchical church or a great diversity of authorities among churches that "the Christian community" seems a better term.

What I shall attempt to do in this chapter is to give some indication as to the grounds of difference in the authority of churches, then make some suggestions as to the uses and misuses of creeds and articles of faith, and end with some observations as to the possibilities of a theology of the Christian community both definitive and unchained.

1. *The nature of the Church*

So commonly do we talk about "the Church," and so naturally do Christians assume that it is simply a composite name for the churches—or, at least, of the churches of their own kind—that its nature may seem on the surface to present no problem. There are many local congregations; there are many denominations; put them all together and you get the Church! The ecumenical Church then becomes the world-wide fellowship of Christians in churches, related to one another through the World Council of Churches.

But the problem is by no means so simple as this. Not only are there many within the ecumenical movement who will tell you that there is no such thing as an "ecumenical church," but there is the persistent fact that the Roman Catholic Church, a major American Protestant denomination (the Southern Baptist Convention), and many smaller denominations and sects are not at all connected with the ecumenical movement and do not want to be. Are we to say that these groups are not part of the Church? Or ought they to say, as the Roman Catholic Church does and the Eastern Orthodox comes near to saying, that only their own household of faith is in a true sense the Church? It may be remembered that at Toronto in 1950, the World Council of Churches came perilously near to splitting apart over questions of ecclesiology raised by Orthodox members of the Central Committee, and that at Evanston in 1954 the same group refused to assent to a call to repentance over the sin of division (since their church as the mystical Body of Christ cannot sin) or to a call to move toward unity (since the Orthodox Church alone is the repository of divine truth).

As a matter of fact, the question as to what constitutes the Church is the deepest division in the present ecumenical movement, and the element in its theology least agreed upon. It is the primary concern of its Faith and Order division.

While some progress has been made at the successive Faith and Order world conferences at Lausanne, Edinburgh, and Lund and at Amsterdam and Evanston in defining the elements of agreement and difference, and while repeated calls to repentance and to greater unity have been uttered, it can scarcely be said that any progress has thus far been made at the point of actual convergence.[1] This is not due to obstinacy, but to deep-seated conviction. What is profoundly believed to be truth cannot be lightly surrendered for the sake of agreement.

It is obviously impossible here even to outline the extensive studies that have been made in this field. The reader is referred to the symposium *The Nature of the Church*, prepared for the Lund Conference under the editorship of R. Newton Flew; to the findings of this conference (Report of the Third World Conference on Faith and Order) ; and to the briefer statements of the Faith and Order sections of the Amsterdam and Evanston conferences. All I can attempt is to indicate the divergent *bases of authority* out of which stem divergent concepts of the nature of the Church, and hence of the authority of its ministry and the validity of its sacraments.

There are three such bases of authority among the churches, tangent to one another at some points, all sincerely professing to stem from Christ, yet so different that different types of churches are constituted by them.

The most distinctive and inflexible of these bases of authority is the so-called "Catholic" position, which those not standing within it are quick to point out is the least catholic from the standpoint of inclusiveness. It is more often referred to by those outside it as the "apostolic succession" or

[1] There have been important mergers, as in the bringing together of three Methodist churches to form one in 1939 and the establishment of the Church of South India in 1947. What is here referred to is the overcoming of theological differences to move toward greater agreement.

"historic episcopate" position. It embraces not only the Roman Catholic Church, but the Greek Catholic and other Eastern Orthodox churches, the Old Catholic,[2] and the Anglo-Catholic wing of the Anglican Church.[3] To this point of view, the Christian Church owes its origin and its authority to its having been constituted by Christ's commission to Peter as recorded in the sixteenth chapter of Matthew, and no church is truly a church, no minister or priest validly ordained, and hence no sacrament really a sacrament, unless its ministry has been ordained by the laying on of hands of a bishop who stands in this historic succession. Intercommunion with other Christians outside this succession therefore becomes impossible, and a sacrilege if practiced.

A second basis of authority is sometimes called by way of contrast the "Protestant," although since, as we shall see, the third group is Protestant also, the term ought not to be thus limited.[4] It might more accurately be called "Reformation Protestant." Its main focus for the individual Christian is the experience of salvation through justification by faith. True to the Reformation emphasis on the Bible as the source both of truth and of spiritual power, it makes much of the preaching of the Word, and the sacraments (now two in number rather than seven) are regarded as vital means of grace though not the sole channels of salvation. A church therefore becomes a congregation of faithful people in

[2] A group which broke with Roman Catholicism by refusing to accept the dogma of papal infallibility when it was promulgated in 1870. Its ritual and sacraments are those of the Roman Catholic Church.

[3] The Anglican Church, with its American correlate, the Protestant Episcopal, holds generally to the historic episcopate but with varying degrees of rigidity. It is therefore both "Catholic" and "Protestant."

[4] The Faith and Order section of the Amsterdam Conference defined the nature of the Church as either "Catholic" or "Protestant" in the Reformation sense, and the third group would have been left out altogether except for protest from the floor of the Assembly. It appears, therefore, somewhat as an afterthought, but was never fully amalgamated into the Report. See *Man's Disorder and God's Design*, Vol. I, pp. 204 ff.

which the Word is purely preached and the sacraments duly
administered. The Lutheran, the Presbyterian, and the
various other Reformed churches stand within this tradition.

Are these all? Some would say so, compressing all other
types of Protestantism into the second group. Yet, as was
pointed out at Amsterdam by Douglas Horton when it was
about to be overlooked, there is a third type which may be
called "the gathered community." The emphasis here is on
personal response to the call of God to become a Christian,
or to accept the responsibilities of Christian discipleship if
one has grown up within Christian nurture, and then to
affiliate voluntarily with others in the fellowship of the
Christian congregation. It does not repudiate the doctrine
of justification by faith, but instead of making this focal it
stresses personal decision, personal commitment to the Christian life, voluntary association with other Christians for
mutual support and for the doing of the works of Christ.
The presence of the Holy Spirit, vivifying the Christian life
and leading quickened minds into fresh apprehensions of
Christian truth, is the source of continuity within the Church
rather than the historic episcopate or a particular doctrine or
ecclesiastical structure.[5]

The clearest example of this third group is the Congrega-
tional Christian Churches. With varying emphases, however, it embraces the Methodists, Baptists, Disciples, and many
smaller denominations including the Pentecostals. Theological liberals, conservatives, and fundamentalists are found
within it, possibly also some neo-orthodox though most of
the latter stem from the Lutheran or Reformed tradition. It
is the dominant view of the Church within American Protestantism, though it is a minority position in the leadership
of the World Council, where Anglican, Lutheran, Reformed,
and Orthodox groups predominate. This fact may throw

[5] For further analysis of this third type see Angus Dun, *Prospecting for
a United Church,* chap. vi.

some light on the theological tensions between American and European Christianity within that body, softened by interchange of thought and fellowship but not yet fully resolved.

But what have these divergent views about the nature and the locus of authority of the Church to do with the problem of this book, the approach to Christian knowledge?

The connection is intangible, with so many crosscurrents that it is difficult, if not impossible, to locate it in specific categories without the making of frequent exceptions. Yet the connection is unmistakably there. One does not have to move in ecumenical circles long before he senses it, whether in written documents from the various traditions or in discussion at an assembly. When one from the "Catholic" tradition speaks, one comes to expect that the Church will be appealed to as the custodian of Christian truth, and that whether or not it is explicitly so stated, it is the apostolically commissioned and apostolically continued church that is *the Church* and there must be no tinkering with its orders, sacraments, or creeds. When one from the Lutheran or Reformed tradition speaks, one expects an appeal to the Bible—an appeal which in spite of the most advanced historical scholarship not infrequently seems to many of the third group too literalistic. Not only the insistence on Christ's second coming, which dominated the Evanston discussions, but also the insistence, stemming from a seminar in Basel, that the statement on the Christian hope contain the prophecy of and a special appeal for the conversion of the Jews, are cases in point.[6] And when one from "the gathered community" speaks, with his presuppositions mainly those of the life and teachings of Jesus, the leading of the Holy Spirit in the present situation, and the duties of Christian disciple-

[6] The attempt to include this was defeated, but by a narrow margin and in a vote in which questions of political and diplomatic expediency were mixed with theology.

ship, it is likely to sound like Christian common sense to his compatriots and like "American activism" to others!

2. The place of creeds

In this brief survey of differing bases of authority within the Christian community I have only incidentally referred to variant attitudes toward the creeds of the Church. This I shall not attempt to trace in detail, but some general observations can be made. To those in the "Catholic" group, the historic Apostles' and Nicene Creeds are second only to the historic episcopate as the bond of connection and guarantor of continuity between the early church and the present. They are a natural part of the ritual of worship inherited from the past, and while they blend with the mood of worship rather than theological analysis by being chanted rather than spoken, their theological validity is seldom questioned.

Among those of the second group there is a strong "confessional" emphasis. In the repudiation of the Roman Catholic confessional as preparatory to penance and priestly absolution, the term assumes a radically different connotation in stress upon "confessions of faith." Nor does this term mean simply the public statement of desire to be a Christian, as in many churches of the third type one joins the church on confession of faith. It means this, but in addition a codified body of theological doctrine wrought out in the early stages of the denomination's history and henceforth regarded as normative, as in the Augsburg, Westminster, and Heidelberg confessions. These, with the Apostles' Creed and connotations derived from long-continued emphasis, are implicitly the bases from which the Bible is interpreted, though explicitly the Bible is held to be the sole basis of Christian faith and conduct, and the creeds and confessions derivative from it.

In the third group, the main emphasis is on the Christian life and experience. Varying views are held regarding creeds and articles of faith, but these are, for the most part, kept in subordination to the experience of the new birth in Christ, to the witness and guidance of the Holy Spirit, to the doing of works of Christian service, and to the desire to associate with and lead others into the fellowship in Christ which constitutes the Church. The Congregationalists, stressing freedom within fellowship, have no creed, but have a large amount of theological agreement which at various times has been put into words, as in the now widely accepted statement of faith formulated at Kansas City in 1913. The Baptists and Disciples profess to have no creed but the Bible, yet distinctive views as to adult baptism serve the purpose of a creed in providing a normative standard of acceptance into the congregation. The Quakers and the Pentecostals, poles apart in many respects of which silence versus lusty vocal expression is but one, nevertheless meet in a high concern for the Holy Spirit and a minor interest in theological distinctions. Within most of the churches of this third group, and to a considerable extent in the second also, cleavages between fundamentalists and liberals within a denomination cut deeper than do the lines of distinction between denominations.

Methodism stands in a somewhat distinctive category. It is "confessional" to the point of having twenty-five articles of faith taken over by John Wesley from the Anglican thirty-nine; and unlike everything else in the *Discipline,* these and the General Rules may not be changed by General Conference action. There is, however, nothing to prevent their reinterpretation. The Apostles' Creed is widely used in Methodist services, but so are two other creeds expressing our common faith in terms more congenial to contemporary understanding. When in the masterful Episcopal Address of 1952, twelve paragraphs were devoted to the statement of what Methodists believe, it is safe to assume that this statement met a warmer response in the hearts and minds of most

Methodists than is often elicited by the Twenty-five Articles.

From this point on, I shall make no attempt to speak except from the standpoint of the freedom granted by my own church to its members and professors of theology. What, then, may a member of a free church[7] believe about the uses and abuses of creeds?

First, we ought to respect them. The most familiar of them, the Apostles' Creed, would not have come down to us over the centuries if it had not been the carrier of something worth respecting. The Nicene Creed, less familiar to most of those of the free-church tradition, still has a wealth of beauty and dignity and Christian meaning. This is not to say they ought to be respected simply because they are old. Some ancient practices, such as foot washing or the veneration of relics, may well be surrendered. But the creeds are a bond between us in the present and our Christian heritage. What was meaningful in the second or the fourth century with regard to the Father, Son, and Holy Spirit is still meaningful, though we may think in different categories and require new modes of expression.

Second, we must understand them. The better we understand their history, the more clearly we see both what our fathers in the faith were trying to say through them, and wherein they are inadequate as full expressions of Christian faith. The earliest form of the Apostles' Creed appears as a baptismal formula, quoted by Irenaeus about the middle of the second century and by Tertullian a little later. Accretions were added until it assumed its present form in the

[7] The term "free church" has a number of meanings, depending on the context in which it is used. It may mean (1) the opposite of a State church, in which sense all American churches are free churches; or (2) all those outside the apostolic succession, recognizing one another's ministries as valid and therefore in open communion. This embraces group three, the Reformed branch of group two, and some Lutheran churches. Or it may mean (3) those churches not making any creedal requirements for membership, either because they are creedless or because they place the main emphasis elsewhere.

seventh or eighth century. It becomes meaningful, therefore, to discover that the phrases introduced by "born of the
Virgin Mary" were not put there to attest Christ's divinity,
which was not in dispute, but to affirm his full humanity
against the heresy of the docetists, who denied it. The "resurrection of the body" did not raise for those early Christians
the scientific problems it inevitably does for us; it simply
meant that God was able to take care of and give eternal life
to the whole being of the Christian who put his trust in Him.
Even a term so easily explained as "the holy catholic church"
is, regrettably, allowed too often to connote the Roman
Catholic Church when it would be a simple matter to show
that it means the divinely grounded, universal Christian
fellowship to which Christ calls his followers, and of which
we are a part.

Third, we ought not to tinker with the creeds. Reinterpret
them we must, and supplement them we must. But if we are
going to use them at all in a service of public worship, let us
use them as they are. The change from "Holy Ghost" to
"Holy Spirit" has been made by the Church as both more
meaningful and more accurate, and is legitimate. But to try
to pull out a phrase here and inject one there is like trying
to make over a Bach chorale or fiddle with one of Raphael's
paintings. The result is a hodgepodge and a mess!

Fourth, let us say them, unless conscience forbids, as an
act of worship and of alignment with our great Christian
past. If one feels that he cannot conscientiously use the Apostles' or the Nicene Creed because it expresses meanings that
he does not share, there are alternatives. But if they are
used, they should be repeated without undue scruples for
what they *stand for,* not necessarily with assent to the literal
meaning of every phrase. To illustrate, few mature Christians today believe literally that God sits on a great throne
up in the sky, at the right of which sits Jesus, waiting to
come again. Nevertheless, we do believe that Jesus Christ

is Lord of heaven and earth, that judgment is real, and that His coming to those who will receive Him is of tremendous importance to our faith and to the world.

Fifth, let us recognize that no compendium of doctrine inherited from the past says everything. New discoveries of biblical truth and new interpretations of this truth for our human living call both for fresh interpretation of the past and for supplementation in the present. The Apostles' Creed, for example, says nothing about Jesus' central theme, the Kingdom of God, while the Nicene mentions it but incidentally in the phrase, "Whose Kingdom shall have no end." Neither one of them says anything about what Jesus made our primary duty—to love God supremely and our neighbor as ourselves. The Apostles' Creed makes no reference to the Bible; the Nicene says only that Jesus rose again according to the Scriptures. The Apostles' Creed mentions—but barely mentions—the Holy Spirit. The Nicene calls the Holy Ghost "the Lord, and Giver of Life, Who proceedeth from the Father and the Son; Who with the Father and Son together is worshipped and glorified; Who spake by the Prophets." But with all these words it does not tell us as much about the relation of the Holy Spirit to our lives as we need to know. It is therefore appropriate that modern creeds—not simply individual credos but those given corporate authority by a church—should be used along with the historic affirmations of our faith.

If the foregoing principles are accepted, a final one must follow from them. This is that no inherited creed, however time-honored and filled with both truth and Christian feeling, should be an instrument of constraint. Creedal tests become dangerous, whether imposed for church membership or for acceptance into the ministry of Christ. This is not to say, as is often too lightly said, that "it makes no difference what you believe so long as you live up to it." It makes a vast difference what a Christian believes. But to insist that a

147

Christian who is earnestly seeking to be responsive to the
call of Christ, to follow the leading of the Holy Spirit, and
to use his God-given mental faculties to discern the truth,
must come out exactly where the historic creeds have placed
their affirmations is to deny any fresh approach to truth
through living experience. "Where the Spirit of the Lord is,
there is freedom," says Paul (II Cor. 3:17), and this is the only
ground on which creeds may be safely used as supports and
not as shackles to Christian faith.

3. *The Word of God in living language*

Where, then, rests our final authority?

We have been canvassing in this study a number of the
most commonly followed pathways to the knowledge of God
and Christian truth. Each one has something to offer, but
none is definitive and complete. Philosophy calls us to think
consistently and with open-minded inquiry about the meaning of life as a whole, and Christian experience is a part of
that whole; yet it leaves us with "the hunger of natural religion." Science presents a vast and ever-growing array of
evidence pointing in the direction of a Supreme Mind and
Cosmic Creator; yet it does not give us "the great companion
—the fellow-sufferer who understands." [8] Revelation can be
and must be co-ordinated with all the general presuppositions of knowledge, which means that faith and reason must
walk together—but how? The Bible is our common Christian heritage, and all theology truly Christian must be
grounded in it, but the Bible obviously requires interpretation, and the interpreters do not agree. If, either in dis-
couragement at lack of certainty from these channels or in
the quickening of the inner life, one turns to the Holy Spirit
for authority, again we are confronted with the problem of
variant voices among equally sincere Christians. Looking

[8] A. N. Whitehead, *Process and Reality*, p. 532.

then for some corporate witness as a tether for our faith, we find great compendiums in the creeds of Christendom, yet there is little that has been believed among Christians, *semper, ubique, ab omnibus.* Are we not left, then, for each man to make up his own mind or, at best, for each church to go its own way, with no attempt at unity?

The foregoing facts may be admitted, and that necessary freedom postulated which must be present where the Spirit of the Lord is, and yet the conclusion of ineptitude and defeat need not be drawn. For there is one thing on which all Christians are agreed! If they are not agreed upon it, they may be competent philosophers or altruistic persons, but they are not Christians. This one "article of religion" was enough for the early Christians, and all the creed they had in those dramatic, Spirit-filled days of the founding of the Church. It has been at the heart of the Christian community ever since, insofar as this has remained truly Christian. Though its ramifications are infinite, it can be understood and accepted by the humblest and most untutored Christian, as it has been through the centuries and is today. It can be stated in three words, *Jesus is Lord!*

This is the one common center of the ecumenical movement, and the ground of any ecumenical theology. The theme of the Faith and Order section of the Evanston Assembly of the World Council of Churches was "Our Oneness in Christ and Our Disunity as Churches." Unity in a common devotion to Christ as Head of the Church and in a common fellowship in Christ across the most disparate cultural and ecclesiastical as well as theological divisions is our common bond. This is seldom disputed. And we may go further and say that in Jesus Christ as Lord lies our final authority in the quest for Christian truth.

This is not to say that Christological formulations of what is meant by "Jesus as Lord" will all come out at the same place. The contrary is obvious, as both the acute controversies of the early church and the variations in Christology today attest.[9] But that Jesus Christ should be accepted as the fountainhead of both Christian truth and Christian experience—this is another matter. Without this conviction, Christian faith loses its identity to become philosophy, ethics, cultic practice, ecclesiastical domination, or simply a vestigial relic of a bygone day. With its acceptance by both mind and heart, other great certainties regarding God, man, the Spirit, the Kingdom, our salvation here and our eternal destiny are assured.

The implications of this faith for other aspects of Christian truth are manifold. It will take not only another book, but books, to state them, and we shall not attempt here to open up these many issues. It must suffice to say here that "the mind of Christ" is our ultimate authority, and to "have this mind among yourselves, which you have in Christ Jesus" is the solvent which breaks down walls of division both in theology and in practice within the inclusive community of Christ's Body. With this mind we shall hear God speaking; without it the voice of the Spirit will be lost in the tumultuous utterances of our time.

The Word of God, we saw, means "God speaking" or "God's self-disclosure." There is a valid sense in which the Bible is the Word of God. God speaks also in the eternal *logos,* the spirit of wisdom and truth discernible in all nature and throughout the total stream of history. Yet God speaks most clearly, unequivocally, unmistakably, in "the Word made flesh" to dwell among us. It is when we behold His glory, full of grace and truth, that we *know*—and are led from this vision to the fashioning of theologies which will always be partial but need not be false apprehensions of God's truth.

[9] For a survey of both historic and contemporary Christologies with a constructive interpretation, the best source is Donald Baillie's *God Was in Christ. In This Name* by Claude Welch gives a survey of views of the Trinity in modern theology.

This vision of God must be recaptured afresh in every generation, caught from the past through the light shed by torches of long ago and carried from generation to generation by the Christian community. It must flame anew in every age through a living synthesis of faith and reason, a personal encounter wherein God in Christ becomes real and is again made flesh to dwell among us. The Word of God must be a living language, or it is not any word at all.

When the Word does thus become a living language through our Lord Jesus Christ—"our Lord" not in name only but in reality and power—than all the rest of the approaches to Christian truth take on new validity and potency. Philosophy leaves the "ivory tower" where not all but too many philosophers dwell, and becomes a clean-cutting instrument whereby to separate the true from the false in our doctrines of God, of man, of the moral life, of our temporal and eternal destiny. The approach through nature, whether physical or human nature—that is, through all the avenues accessible to the procedures of empirical science— becomes no longer the sole access to knowledge or a rival of Christian faith, but its reinforcement. Nature does not of itself lead us to Christ; yet Christ transfigures all nature. When seen through His eyes, there is nothing small in all God's world.

With our Lord Jesus Christ as supreme revelation, much that otherwise seems common, even unclean, becomes revelatory. One sees the handiwork of His Father in the vast expanses of the heavens, but also in common things like birds and lilies, fishing nets and lost sheep, "the least of these my brethren." In the light of His revealing love, every human soul takes on infinite worth, and we are led not only to faith but to service. In a living synthesis of faith and reason, love becomes the capstone of the whole.

The Bible embraces many things. It contains important sociological data as to the advance of a tenacious people from a patriarchal society to monarchy and its decline, from henotheism to ethical monotheism, from primitivism to an advanced culture. It is a library of great literature—the world's greatest, as continued record-breaking sales attest. But above all, the Bible when read in faith is the Word of God. And it is this because the Word made flesh imparts meaning to it all. The Old Testament *can* be read without the New; it is not meaningless without it, as its precious character to our Jewish friends gives evidence. But when the Old Testament is read in the light of the New, and the whole is seen in the light of that "light of the world" which came in Jesus Christ, it takes on a validity and a vitality it could not have without it, and that no textual or historical scrutiny alone could give it. It becomes living language because it has a living center.

The Holy Spirit is the Spirit of God with and within us, and this means in the Christian structure of thought the presence of the Living Christ. Though problems must remain as to just the point at which the voice of our own thought and impulse is stilled and the Voice of the Lord speaks, we are not left without guidance. It is when we have the mind of Christ as our frame of reference, and can square the impulses that come to us against the man our Lord was and the words He spoke and the deeds He did, that we can be sure the Holy Spirit still speaks today.

And what of the Christian community? To one who stands outside the Church it is apt to seem tradition-bound, if not archaic, at best a dignified social institution, at worst an enemy of progress. To one who stands within it, even when the familiar ties are close-binding it is apt to be but little more than a place to go habitually on Sunday mornings. But to the churchman who is at the same time deeply and intelligently Christian, the Church is that fellowship wherein our Lord Jesus Christ is most truly known, His work most fully done, His gospel most faithfully carried to a needy world.

Within this fellowship it is not a matter of argument or of interesting speculation but of *knowledge* that Christ is the hope of the world.

So, it comes about that we need not be left to grope as to the foundations of Christian knowledge. It is true, as sung by many millions of Christians, that

> The Church's one foundation
> Is Jesus Christ her Lord.

It is also true that the one indispensable, unshakable foundation of our knowledge of God and of all God's relations with our world is the living incarnation of God in our Lord Jesus Christ.

When we have finished our theologizing, we shall not understand all mysteries. We are but human pilgrims following the pathways of knowledge, and to the end of the earthly way we shall still "know in part." Yet our faith in Jesus Christ our Lord can give us the *assurance* of things hoped for, the *conviction* of things not seen. And is not that, after all, the object of the quest?

Selected Bibliography

A. General References

Baillie, John. *Our Knowledge of God.* New York: Charles Scribner's Sons, 1939.

Barth, Karl. *The Doctrine of the Word of God.* New York: Charles Scribner's Sons, 1936.

Brunner, H. Emil. *Revelation and Reason.* Philadelphia: Westminster Press, 1946.

DeWolf, L. Harold. *A Theology of the Living Church,* Parts I, II. New York: Harper & Bros., 1953.

Ferré, Nels F. S. *Faith and Reason.* New York: Harper & Bros., 1946.

Horton, Walter M. *Christian Theology: An Ecumenical Approach.* New York: Harper & Bros., 1955.

Jones, Rufus M. *Pathways to the Reality of God.* New York: The Macmillan Co., 1931.

Knudson, Albert C. *The Doctrine of God,* Part I. New York and Nashville: Abingdon Press, 1930.

Lyman, Eugene W. *The Meaning and Truth of Religion.* New York: Charles Scribner's Sons, 1933.

Macintosh, D. C. *The Problem of Religious Knowledge.* New York: Harper & Bros., 1940.

Rall, Harris Franklin. *Christianity: An Inquiry into Its Nature and Truth.* New York: Charles Scribner's Sons, 1940.

Ramsdell, Edward T. *The Christian Perspective.* New York and Nashville: Abingdon Press, 1950.

Richardson, Alan. *Christian Apologetics.* New York: Harper & Bros., 1947.

———. *The Gospel and Modern Thought.* New York: Oxford University Press, 1950.

Temple, William. *Nature, Man and God.* New York: The Macmillan Co., 1934.

Tillich, Paul. *Systematic Theology,* Vol. I, Part I. Chicago: University of Chicago Press, 1951.

B. On Special Topics

(Arranged according to chapters)

I. *Authority in Christian Belief*
See above list; also the following surveys of Christian theology written primarily for laymen.

Bosley, Harold A. *A Firm Faith for Today.* New York: Harper & Bros., 1950.

Ferré, Nels F. S. *Pillars of Faith.* New York: Harper & Bros., 1948.

Gray, Henry David. *A Theology for Christian Youth.* New York and Nashville: Abingdon Press, 1941.

Harkness, Georgia. *Understanding the Christian Faith.* New York and Nashville: Abingdon Press, 1947.

Harner, Nevin C. *I Believe.* Philadelphia: Christian Education Press, 1950.

Hordern, William. *A Layman's Guide to Protestant Theology.* New York: The Macmillan Co., 1955.

Horton, Walter M. *Our Christian Faith.* Boston: Pilgrim Press, 1945.

Nichols, James H. *Primer for Protestants.* New York: Association Press, 1947.

Selected Bibliography

Rall, Harris Franklin. *A Faith for Today.* New York and Nashville: Abingdon Press, 1936.

Sockman, Ralph W. *How to Believe.* Garden City: Doubleday & Co., 1953.

Spurrier, William A. *A Guide to the Christian Faith.* New York: Charles Scribner's Sons, 1952.

Whale, John S. *Christian Doctrine.* New York: The Macmillan Co., 1941.

II. *Philosophy and Theology*

Bertocci, Peter A. *Introduction to the Philosophy of Religion.* New York: Prentice-Hall, 1951.

Brightman, Edgar S. *A Philosophy of Religion.* New York: Prentice-Hall, 1940.

Casserley, J. V. L. *The Christian in Philosophy.* New York: Charles Scribner's Sons, 1951.

DeWolf, L. Harold. *The Religious Revolt Against Reason.* New York: Harper & Bros., 1949.

Gilson, Etienne. *God and Philosophy.* New Haven: Yale University Press, 1941.

Harkness, Georgia. *Conflicts in Religious Thought.* Rev. ed. New York: Harper & Bros., 1949.

Hocking, William Ernest. *The Meaning of God in Human Experience.* New Haven: Yale University Press, 1912.

Lewis, Edwin. *A Philosophy of the Christian Revelation.* New York: Harper & Bros., 1940.

Macintosh, D. C. *The Reasonableness of Christianity.* New York: Charles Scribner's Sons., 1925.

Tennant, Frederick R. *Philosophical Theology.* 2 vols. New York: The Macmillan Co., 1928, 1930.

Trueblood, D. Elton. *The Knowledge of God.* New York: Harper & Bros., 1939.

———. *The Logic of Belief.* New York: Harper & Bros., 1942.

Wieman, Henry Nelson. *The Wrestle of Religion with Truth.* New York: The Macmillan Co., 1927.

———. *The Source of Human Good.* Chicago: University of Chicago Press, 1946.

III. *Theology and Scientific Method*

Brightman, Edgar S. *Nature and Values.* New York and Nashville: Abingdon Press, 1945.

Du Noüy, Lecomte. *Human Destiny.* New York: Longmans, Green & Co., 1947.

Eddington, Arthur S. *Science and the Unseen World.* New York: The Macmillan Co., 1929.

Harkness, Georgia. *The Recovery of Ideals,* Chs. VIII-XI. New York: Charles Scribner's Sons, 1937.

Hocking, William Ernest. *Science and the Idea of God.* Chapel Hill: University of North Carolina Press, 1944.

Horton, Walter M. *Theism and the Scientific Spirit.* New York: Harper & Bros., 1933.

Macintosh, D. C. *Theology as an Empirical Science.* New York: The Macmillan Co., 1919.

Mather, Kirtley F. *Science in Search of God.* New York: Henry Holt & Co., 1928.

Wieman, Henry Nelson. *Religious Experience and Scientific Method.* New York: The Macmillan Co., 1926.

IV. *Revelation, Faith, and Knowledge*

All of the books listed under "General References" deal with this problem. Note also the following:

Baillie, John and Hugh Martin, eds. *Revelation.* New York: The Macmillan Co., 1937. (An ecumenical symposium).

Niebuhr, H. Richard. *The Meaning of Revelation.* New York: The Macmillan Co., 1941.

Robinson, H. Wheeler. *Redemption and Revelation,* Part II. New York: Harper & Bros., 1942.

Scott, Ernest F. *The New Testament Idea of Revelation.* New York: Charles Scribner's Sons, 1935.

Streeter, B. H. *The God Who Speaks.* New York: The Macmillan Co., 1936.

V. *The Authority of the Bible*

Anderson, Bernhard. *Rediscovering the Bible.* New York: Association Press, 1951.

Burrows, Millar. *An Outline of Biblical Theology.* Philadelphia: Westminster Press, 1946.

Chase, Mary Ellen. *The Bible and the Common Reader.* New York: The Macmillan Co., 1944.

Dodd, C. H. *The Authority of the Bible.* New York: Harper & Bros., 1929.

Fosdick, Harry Emerson. *The Modern Use of the Bible.* New York: The Macmillan Co., 1924.

———. *A Guide to the Understanding of the Bible.* New York: Harper & Bros., 1938.

Harkness, Georgia. *Toward Understanding the Bible.* New York: Charles Scribner's Sons, 1954.

Knox, John. *Criticism and Faith.* New York and Nashville: Abingdon Press, 1952.

Richardson, Alan. *A Preface to Bible-Study.* Philadelphia: Westminster Press, 1944.

Richardson, Alan and Wolfgang Schweitzer, eds. *Biblical Authority for Today.* Philadelphia: Westminster Press, 1952.

Rowley, H. H. *The Relevance of the Bible.* New York: The Macmillan Co., 1944.

Watts, Harold H. *The Modern Reader's Guide to the Bible.* New York: Harper & Bros., 1949.

VI. *The Inner Light of the Spirit*

Bergson, Henri. *The Two Sources of Morality and Religion.* New York: Henry Holt & Co., 1935.

Brightman, Edgar S. *The Spiritual Life.* New York and Nashville: Abingdon Press, 1942.

Hocking, William Ernest. *The Meaning of God in Human Experience,* Parts V, VI. New Haven: Yale University Press, 1912.

SELECTED BIBLIOGRAPHY

Inge, W. R. *Christian Mysticism.* New York: Charles Scribner's Sons, 1899, 1933.

James, William. *Varieties of Religious Experience,* Lectures XI-XVII. New York: Longmans, Green & Co., 1902.

Jones, Rufus M. *Studies in Mystical Religion.* New York: The Macmillan Co., 1909; *New Studies in Mystical Religion,* 1927; *The Testimony of the Soul,* 1936; and many others.

Kepler, Thomas S., comp. *The Fellowship of the Saints:* An Anthology of Christian Devotional Literature. New York and Nashville: Abingdon Press, 1948.

Knudson, Albert C. *The Doctrine of Redemption,* Ch. VIII. New York and Nashville: Abingdon Press, 1933.

Otto, Rudolf. *The Idea of the Holy.* London: Oxford University Press, 1928.

Pratt, James B. *The Religious Consciousness,* Chs. XVI-XX. New York: The Macmillan Co., 1920.

Steere, Douglas V. *On Beginning from Within.* New York: Harper & Bros., 1943.

Underhill, Evelyn. *Mysticism.* New York: E. P. Dutton & Co., 1911.

VII. *The Authority of the Christian Community*

Amsterdam Assembly Series: *Man's Disorder and God's Design,* Vol. I, "The Universal Church in God's Design." New York: Harper & Bros., 1948.

Bosley, Harold A. *A Firm Faith for Today,* Chs. I, VI. New York: Harper & Bros., 1950.

DeWolf, L. Harold. *A Theology of the Living Church,* Part VI. New York: Harper & Bros., 1952.

Ferré, Nels F. S. *The Christian Fellowship.* New York: Harper & Bros., 1940.

Flew, R. Newton, ed. *The Nature of the Church.* New York: Harper & Bros., 1952. (Preparatory volume for the Lund Conference on Faith and Order.)

Garrison, Winfred E. *A Protestant Manifesto.* New York and Nashville: Abingdon Press, 1952.

Knudson, Albert C. *The Doctrine of Redemption,* Ch. IX. New York and Nashville: Abingdon Press, 1933.

Morrison, C. C. *What Is Christianity?* Chicago: Willett, Clark & Co., 1940.

Newbigin, Lesslie. *The Household of God.* New York: Friendship Press, 1954.

Niebuhr, H. Richard. *The Social Sources of Denominationalism.* New York: Henry Holt & Co., 1929.

Tillich, Paul. *The Protestant Era.* Chicago: University of Chicago Press, 1948.

Index

(Arabic numerals refer to pages; italic Roman numerals to chapters)

158

INDEX

Francis of Assisi, 132
Fundamentalism, 17, 19, 66, 80, 97, 100, 103-4, 106, 108-9, 111, 114, 116, 141, 144

Gladden, Washington, 98
God: doctrine of, 22, 23, 26, 34, 70-71, 87, 129, 150, 151; as personal, 68, 71, 88-90, 105; as revealed through creation, 18, 53, 62-63, 74, 87, 98, 104, 111, 112, 148; *see also* Grace; Jesus Christ; Word
Grace, 78, 81, 90, 102, 110, 114, 122, 132, 135, 140
Greek philosophy, 36, 40, 64, 105

Heilsgeschichte, 110, 114, 116
Herrmann, Wilhelm, 81
Historic episcopate, 140-43
Holy Spirit, 117-26, 136, 141, 142, 144, 146, 150, 152; interpreter of the Word, 79, 102; witness of, 51, 112, 120, 135
Horton, Douglas, 141
Horton, Walter M., 67
Humanism, 23-24, 70, 74, 98, 105, 127
Huxley, Julian, 74

Idealism, philosophical, 44, 48, 55
Ignatius, 101
Incarnation, 34, 76, 91, 104, 150, 153
Intuition, 43, 45
Irenaeus, 145

James, William, 132
Jesus Christ, 15, 26, 34, 39, 92, 108, 115, 118, 146, 150; as final authority, 91-92, 148-53; life and teachings of, 22, 62, 99, 106, 119, 121-22, 123; redemption by, 98, 101-2, 112, 114, 115, 125; revelation of God in, 56, 75, 82, 84, 87, 88, 91-92, 93, 101, 110, 111-12, 129, 151; second coming, 17, 103, 112, 142, 146, 151
John of the Cross, 132
Jones, Rufus M., 130, 131, 133
Justin Martyr, 15, 36 n.

Kant, Immanuel, 55
Kingdom of God, 63, 99, 105, 111, 147, 150
Knudson, Albert C., 98

Lawrence, Brother, 62
Liberalism, 17, 19, 44, 53, 66, 98-100, 103, 104-10, 115-16, 141, 144; changes in, 15, 25, 97; and neo-orthodoxy, 44, 110-14; secular, 104-5, 113
Lippmann, Walter, 15
Logic, 29, 35, 46
Logos, 36, 56, 150
Loisy, A. F., 99

Luther, Martin, 97, 102
Lyman, Eugene W., 37

Macintosh, D. C., 37
Man, doctrine of, 26, 34, 68, 98, 111, 150, 151
Materialism, 23, 68
Mathematics, 46, 52
Melanchthon, Philip, 102
Metaphysics, 12, 14, 29-30, 34, 35, 39, 44, 48, 50
Mind and nature, 48-49, 93, 94
Miracle, 53, 88, 90-91, 99
Modernism, 99, 103
Mysticism, 45, 51, 69, 70-71, 117, 128, 130-35
Myth, 112-13

Naturalism, 23-24, 26, 68, 70-72; religious, 66, 71, 105
Nature, as revelation of God, 86, 92, 94, 98, 106, 111, 151
Neo-orthodoxy, 15, 19, 20, 25, 36, 67, 82, 85, 100, 103, 104, 106, 110-14, 115, 135, 141; reasons for emergence of, 17, 44, 66, 98-99; *see also* Liberalism
Newman, John Henry, 16
Nicene Creed, 143, 145, 146, 147
Niebuhr, H. Richard, 85
Niebuhr, Reinhold, 67, 97, 113
Normative sciences, 29, 52

Objectivity: of religious experience, 58, 75-76, 84, 94; of truth, 21, 47-48, 93, 94
Origen, 15
Orwell, George, 55
Outler, Albert, 63

Pantheism, 71, 134
Paradox, 44-45
Paul, 18, 113, 114, 118, 122, 124, 126, 130, 148
Pentecost, 15, 119, 121-25, 137
Peter, 15, 121, 124, 140
Philosophical theology, 32-33, 34, 36, 41, 50, 93, 95, 100
Philosophy, *II*, 74, 77-79, 105; contributions to theology, 39-42, 92-94, 148, 151; meaning and aims, 28-31; in tension with theology, 23, 35-39, 150
Philosophy of religion, 33, 34, 35, 75, 137
Plato, 29, 31, 36, 112
Positivism, 23, 26, 68, 69-70
Pragmatic test, 43, 45
Prayer, 26, 65, 126-30, 133-34
Presuppositions of knowledge, 42-50, 92-94, 95, 128, 148
Protestantism, 18, 77, 79-80, 82, 98, 102, 110, 138, 140

159